rororo

rororo

**rororo Sprachen**

Herausgegeben von Ludwig Moos

Sicherheit im aktiven Gebrauch des Englischen gewinnen wir nur, wenn wir die unentbehrlichen Redemittel und typischen Redewendungen problemlos abrufen können. Zum Glück behält unser Gedächtnis kurze Sprachmodule genauso leicht wie ein einzelnes Wort. *Master Your Phrases*, zum Nachschlagen und Lernen gleichermaßen geeignet, schlüsselt die wichtigsten Wendungen der englischen Alltags- und Umgangssprache auf. Mir einem ausgefeilten, nach Schwierigkeiten gestuften Trainingsprogramm vermittelt es die Fertigkeit, der Sprache Struktur zu geben. Ein Verzeichnis nach Situationen erlaubt den gezielten Zugriff auf passende Wendungen.

Dr. René Bosewitz ist *native speaker* und leitet eine Sprachschule in Heidelberg. Robert Kleinschroth unterrichtet Englisch am Gymnasium.

Von René Bosewitz ist bei rororo sprachen *Better Your English* (60802) und *Perfect Your English* (61147) erschienen. Robert Kleinschroth hat unter anderem *Sprachen lernen* (60842), *Flüssiges Französisch* (61184, zusammen mit Anne-Laure und Dieter Maupai) veröffentlicht. Beide zusammen haben *Joke Your Way Through English Grammar* (61408) und *Joke by Joke to Conversation* (18797) geschrieben und die Serie *Business English* konzipiert.

René Bosewitz / Robert Kleinschroth

# Master Your Phrases

Der Schlüssel zum sicheren Englisch

Rowohlt Taschenbuch Verlag

**Originalausgabe**
Veröffentlicht im Rowohlt Taschenbuch Verlag GmbH, Reinbek bei Hamburg, April 2002

Umschlagillustration Gerd Huss
**Gestaltung** Anne Drude
**Satz** Stone, PostScript Linotype Library, QuarkXPress 3.31
**Druck und Bindung** Clausen & Bosse, Leck
Printed in Germany
ISBN 3 499 61334 4

# The Contents

# Preface – Vorwort

Sie haben dieses Buch aufgeschlagen, weil Sie sich für die englische Sprache interessieren. Sie fragen sich: „Lohnt es sich? Ist es das Richtige für mich?" Urteilen Sie selbst.

- *Master Your Phrases* ist ein Nachschlage-, Lern- und Arbeitsbuch der englischen Alltags- und Umgangssprache. Sie lernen Englisch fürs Gespräch.
- Sie sichern und testen Ihre *phrases* schnell mit zahlreichen und originellen *Quick checks*. Bei diesen Schnelltests haben wir Wert auf Kürze, Abwechslung und Vielfalt gelegt.
- Sie lernen keine Einzelwörter, keine Grammatikregeln, sondern *words in context*, idiomatischen Wortschatz, ganze Ausdrücke und Sätze, also das Substantiv mit seinem treffenden Verb und der zugehörigen Präposition.
- Sie lernen im Zusammenhang. Die fünfzehn Kapitel fächern sich in weit über hundert Unterthemen und Situationen auf. Mit dem *Bird's eye view* haben Sie einen schnellen Überblick über das Kapitel, der *Pathfinder* erlaubt Ihnen den gezielten Zugriff auf Redewendungen zu bestimmten Themen und Situationen.
- Das Besondere: Jedes Kapitel ist in zwei Niveaus unterteilt. *Level 1* bietet thematischen Wortschatz in einfachen Sätzen der Alltagssprache. *Level 2* enthält die idiomatischen Redewendungen zum Thema, die *true friends* (*get cold feet*: kalte Füße bekommen) und *false friends* (*be a chicken:* ein Hasenfuß sein).
  Idioms sind mehr als nur das „Sahnehäubchen" auf der Konversation. Viele Idioms sind Sprachfallen für Nicht-Muttersprachler und Ursache für Missverständnisse.

Zur Erholung geben wir Ihnen *Time for a smile* in Form von achtzig Proben angelsächsischen Humors. Unsere Wortschatzhilfen im Anhang erleichtern Ihnen das Verständnis. Noch eins: Das oberste und härteste Gesetz des Lernens lautet: „Lernen tut nur, wer will." Sie wollen lernen, sonst hätten Sie nicht so weit gelesen. Wir wünschen Ihnen dabei viel Erfolg.

# From the cradle to the grave

## *Von der Wiege bis zur Bahre*

1

### Bird's eye view

**LEVEL I**

1. *Das Leben des Boris* – The life of Boris
2. *Du und der Beamte* – You and the civil servant

**LEVEL II**

1. Birth and infancy – *Geburt und Babyjahre*
2. Early childhood – *Frühe Kindheit*
3. School and education – *Schule und Erziehung*
4. Coming of age – *Volljährig werden*
5. Making one's way – *Seinen Weg gehen*
6. Passing away – *Sterben*

### Time for a smile

Boris mother thought that plenty of spinach would put colour in his cheeks. And it did. He was the only kid in the street with green cheeks.

1 **LEVEL 1**

We are born, we get older, we die. Not very philosophical but very true. And all the time we need phrases to describe all these phases of our lives and our feelings. When we are christened, baptised, married (and later divorced) we use special words and phrases. We study, learn a trade and get a job.
We move through our society and in doing so we talk about ourselves. We explain what we do for a living, our likes and dislikes. And for all these things we need phrases. Read on!

## 1. *Das Leben des Boris* – The life of Boris

| | |
|---|---|
| *ein Kind bekommen* | Tina is going to have a baby. She hopes it will be a son. |
| *gebären; zur Welt bringen* | Tina gave birth to a boy. Tom was very happy. |
| *taufen; Taufe* | Tina's and Tom's son was christened Boris. |
| *aufwachsen* | Boris grew up in England and went to school in London. |
| *Erinnerungen an die Kindheit* | Boris has few memories of his childhood. |
| *aufgezogen werden von* | Boris was raised by Tina and her grandmother. |
| *Abitur machen (England)* | After he had passed his A levels, he went to university. |
| *volljährig sein* | When Boris came of age he left home. |
| *verlobt sein* | At the age of 24 Boris was already engaged to Anne. |
| *aus Liebe heiraten* | Boris married Anne for love – he was not interested in her money. |
| *in die Brüche gehen* | In the seventh year their marriage broke up. |
| *sich trennen* | After long and painful quarrels they separated. |
| *sich von jemandem scheiden lassen* | A year later Boris divorced Anne. |
| *seine Verlobung auflösen* | He got engaged to Jill, but soon broke off their engagement. |

| | |
|---|---|
| *in der Blüte der Jahre* | At the age of 50 Boris was in the prime of his life and a wealthy man. |
| *sein Testament machen* | At the age of 70 Boris made his will. |
| *krank werden* | He fell ill and died a week later. |
| *begraben werden* | Boris was buried in a small town near London. |
| *dem Begräbnis beiwohnen* | Only a few old friends attended his funeral. |

## QUICK CHECK 1: Complete the phrases

Ten important events in the life of Boris

| | |
|---|---|
| **1.** He was .................... in a clinic. | **2.** He was ....................... Boris. |
| **3.** He was ..................... by his grandma. | **4.** He ....... ........ love with a girl. |
| **5.** He got *e* ............ *ed.* | **6.** He got *m*............ *ed.* |
| **7.** He was *d* ............ *ed.* | **8.** He fell ................................... |
| **9.** He *d*....... . | **10.** He was *b* ...... *ed.* |

## QUICK CHECK 2: Find the rhyme

In the prime of his _______
Boris met his future wife.

At the age of 70 Boris fell ill.
It was high time to make his _______.

### TIME FOR A SMILE

When Boris was an adolescent the family were so poor they had to share clothes with each other, which wasn't very practical because he had five sisters.

## 2. *Du und der Beamte* – You and the civil servant

| | |
|---|---|
| *Geburtszeugnis* | Can I see your birth certificate, please? |
| *seine Personalien angeben* | At the police station he had to state his particulars / personal data |
| *seinen Namen angeben* | But he refused to give his name. |
| *einen Pass haben* | Which passport do you hold? – I have a German passport. |
| *Staatsangehörigkeit* | What nationality is Tanja? Is she German or French? |
| *Staatsangehörigkeit annehmen* | In 1960 Peter took on French citizenship. |
| *Staatenloser* | What citizenship is Tanja? – She's a stateless person. |
| *Vorname* | What's your first name? – Robert, but you may call me Bob. |
| *Familienname, Zuname* | What's your last name / surname? – Smith, Bob Smith. |
| *Wie alt sind Sie?* | May I ask how old you are? – I'm thirty-nine. |
| *das gleiche Alter haben / gleichaltrig sein* | I'm thirty-nine, too. So we are the same age. |
| *minderjährig sein* | My daughter is still under age. She's sixteen. |
| *Geburtstag haben* | When is your birthday? – My birthday is in July. |
| *geboren sein* | When were you born? – My date of birth is August 12, 1967. |
| *im Pass steht* | In your passport it says that you were born in Munich. |
| *gebürtiger Deutscher* | What nationality are you? – I'm German by birth. |
| *Geschlecht* | What sex is this dog? Is it male or female? |
| *berufstätig sein* | Do you work? – Yes. – And what do you do for a living? |
| *Was sind Sie von Beruf?* | What's your job? – I'm a salesman. |

| | |
|---|---|
| *Firma* | What company do you work for? – I work for Siemens. |
| *geschäftlich hier sein* | Are you here on business? |
| *verheiratet / unverheiratet sein* | Are you married? – No, I'm single. |
| *Geschwister haben* | Have you got any brothers or sisters? |
| *den Totenschein ausstellen* | They've already issued the death certificate. |

## QUICK CHECK 3: How to satisfy civil servants

Which documents do you need to make a civil servant believe that

| | |
|---|---|
| **1.** you were born? | .............................. |
| **2.** you are not a citizen of Iraq? | .............................. |
| **3.** you are dead? | .............................. |

## QUICK CHECK 4: Civil servants ask these questions

| What was the question if this is | your answer? |
|---|---|
| **1.** What is your ............................., sir? | *male* |
| **2.** What is your ............................., sir? | *Boris* |
| **3.** What is your ............................., sir? | *Baker* |
| **4.** What is your ............................., sir? | *German* |
| **5.** What is your ............................., sir? | *35* |
| **6.** What is your marital .......................? | *single* |

### TIME FOR A SMILE

Boris fell down the stairs and was taken to hospital. After examining him, the doctor said, "I have some good news and some bad news for you. First of all, you'll never be able to work again." Boris said, "Okay, now what's the bad news?"

1 LEVEL

We were all born at some time. I first *saw the light of day* in 1949 and a lot of things have changed since then. As a child I had a lot of *teething problems* and I never really got rid of them.
I wasn't a good pupil and I even managed to *get expelled.* And through my working life *I stood on my own two feet,* but I couldn't *toady to* people, which probably means that I'm not very realistic. Perhaps *I'm getting past it.*

## 1. Birth and infancy – *Geburt und Babyjahre*

| | |
|---|---|
| be in labour | *in den Wehen liegen* |
| have labour pains | *Wehenschmerzen haben* |
| have a miscarriage | *eine Fehlgeburt haben* |
| see the light of day | *das Licht der Welt erblicken* |
| from the cradle | *von Kindheit an* |
| be born under a lucky star | *ein Glückskind sein* |
| be endowed with a talent from birth | *ein Talent in die Wiege gelegt bekommen* |
| be born with a silver spoon in one's mouth | *mit einem silbernen Löffel im Mund geboren werden* |
| still be in one's nappies | *noch in den Windeln liegen* |
| still be in its infancy | *(noch) in den Windeln stecken* |
| be born prematurely | *eine Frühgeburt sein* |
| baby boom generation / years | *geburtenstarke Jahrgänge* |
| born with a hearing / sight defect | *mit einer Hör- / Sehschwäche geboren werden* |

TIME FOR A SMILE

A couple walking in the park noticed a young man and woman sitting on a bench, kissing passionately. "Why don't you do that?" said the wife. – "Honey," replied her husband, "I don't even know that woman!"

## 2. Early childhood – *Frühe Kindheit*

| | |
|---|---|
| go potty over children | *ein Kindernarr sein* |
| express something in children's terms | *etwas kindgemäß ausdrücken* |
| baby someone | *jemanden wie ein Baby behandeln* |
| Once bitten twice shy. | *Gebranntes Kind scheut das Feuer.* |
| have teething problems | *Kinderkrankheiten haben* |
| outgrow one's clothes | *aus seinen Kleidern herauswachsen* |
| have no manners | *keine Manieren haben* |
| be well-behaved | *wohlerzogen sein* |
| be well-brought up | *gut erzogen sein* |
| not know right from wrong | *Gut von Böse nicht unterscheiden können* |
| You were young once. | *Du warst auch mal jung.* |

### QUICK CHECK 5: Baby idioms in business

Match the idioms with the definitions.

| | |
|---|---|
| **1.** Don't throw the baby out with the bathwater. | **A.** abandon something that is one's own responsibility and leave it for others to deal with |
| **2.** The whole project is your baby now. | **B.** have minor problems in the early stages of a new project |
| **3.** His business partners were left holding the baby. | **C.** something that one cares about or that one is responsible for |
| **4.** The car still has a few teething problems. | **D.** get rid of something valuable at the same time as one is getting rid of something useless |

### TIME FOR A SMILE

Boris was kissing her at the party when she said: "Am I the first girl you ever had?" He stared at her thoughtfully and answered: "Could be – where were you in 1998?"

1

## QUICK CHECK 6: Idioms overheard

Can you repair the words in *italics*?

In a Chinese restaurant, Bob and Ron; a little boy runs past and kicks Bob's leg. Bob spills his soup:

**B:** Damnation. That child has no *mansern.* He should be disciplined.
**R:** Oh Bob, you were young *enoc* though I can't imagine it.
**B:** Very funny, but it doesn't change the fact that that little boy is *badly hotgurb up*. I tell you what I'd do with him ...

## 3. School and education – *Schule und Erziehung*

| | |
|---|---|
| be the teacher's favourite | *der Liebling des Lehrers sein* |
| get the teacher's back up | *den Lehrer gegen sich aufbringen* |
| become a prefect | *Vertrauensschüler werden* |
| be the school bully | *der Schultyrann sein* |
| join the sixth form | *in die zwölfte Klasse kommen* |
| do one's O-levels / GCEs | *mittlere Reife machen (England)* |
| do one's A-levels | *Abitur machen (England)* |
| play truant | *die Schule schwänzen* |
| give someone a good going-over | *jemanden vertrimmen* |
| get a bad / poor report | *eine schlechtes Zeugnis bekommen* |
| get expelled | *von der Schule fliegen* |
| be put on detention | *nachsitzen (müssen)* |

### TIME FOR A SMILE

The Reverend Mother of a convent school asked each of her ex-pupils what career they had chosen. One of the girls said that she had become a prostitute. The Reverend Mother went pale and nearly fainted. When she had recovered from the shock, she asked the girl to repeat what she had said. "A prostitute," repeated the girl. "Thank God," said the Reverend Mother, "I thought for a moment you said a Protestant."

## 4. Coming of age – *Volljährig werden*

| | |
|---|---|
| cut one's teeth on something | *Erfahrungen bei etwas sammeln* |
| be at a difficult age | *in einem schwierigen Alter sein* |
| a rebellious generation | *ein rebellische Generation* |
| paddle one's own canoe | *auf eigenen Beinen stehen* |
| stand on one's own two feet | *auf eigenen Beinen stehen* |
| have a high opinion of oneself | *eine hohe Meinung von sich haben* |
| not know the difference between right and wrong | *den Unterschied von Gut und Böse nicht kennen* |
| sow one's wild oats | *sich die Hörner abstoßen* |
| be one's hope for the future | *jemandes Hoffnung für die Zukunft sein* |

### QUICK CHECK 7: The early life of Boris

1. Boris was one of the baby .......................... generation.
2. At the age of six he was still in his ...................... .
3. At the age of 14 he was at an ...................... age.
4. At 17 he started to ...................... his wild ...................... .
5. When he came of age he cut his ...................... as a mechanic.
6. Today he designs robots. But they have a lot of ...................... problems.

## 5. Making one's way – *Seinen Weg gehen*

| | |
|---|---|
| be a highflier | *ein Überflieger sein* |
| carve out one's career | *an seiner Karriere schnitzen* |
| pass an exam with flying colours | *eine Prüfung mit Glanz und Gloria bestehen* |
| soft-soap someone | *jemandem Honig um den Bart schmieren* |
| toady to someone | *vor jemandem kriechen; Rad fahren* |
| lick someone's boots | *jemandem die Stiefel lecken* |
| be a creep | *eine Radfahrer sein* |
| be kicked upstairs | *auf das Abstellgleis befördert werden* |
| put someone out to pasture / grass | *aufs Abstellgleis schieben; in den Ruhestand versetzen* |

| | |
|---|---|
| get the golden / leaden handshake | *mit einer fetten / mageren Abfindung abgespeist werden* |
| bite the bullet and try one's best | *die Zähne zusammenbeißen und sein Bestes versuchen* |
| get the axe / boot (sl) | *gefeuert werden* |
| sack / fire / axe someone (sl) | *jemanden feuern / rauswerfen* |
| give someone his cards / walking papers | *jemandem die Papiere geben / ihn entlassen* |

## QUICK CHECK 8: Idioms overheard

What's wrong with the idioms?

**H:** Hi Ron. Nice to see you again after all this time. How's life?

**R:** Grunt, grunt! You try to *cut* out a *career* and you get a smack on the nose.

**H:** It's the same with me. I passed all my exams with *flying flags* and started working. And now after all these years I get *pushed up the stairs.*

**R:** Take it easy, Helmut. At least you've got your health. Not everybody's so lucky.

### TIME FOR A SMILE

***Such is life***

The first half is ruined by your parents. The second half is ruined by your kids.

Life begins at 40, but you could miss a lot if you wait till then.

If I had my life to live over again, I' d start making the same mistakes earlier.

## QUICK CHECK 9: Take a vowel for an x

Each vowel has been replaced by an *x*.

1. Boris was born with a *sxlvxr spxxn* in his mouth.
2. He could read when he was still in his *nxppxxs.*
3. He became a *prxfxct* because he never played *trxxnt.*
4. He tried to *pxddlx* his own *cxnxx* when he was still very young.

## 6. Passing away – *Sterben*

| | |
|---|---|
| get long in the tooth | *alt werden* |
| be shaky on one's feet | *wacklig auf den Füßen sein* |
| be as old as the hills | *steinalt sein* |
| kick the bucket | *abkratzen* |
| die a natural death | *eines natürlichen Todes sterben* |
| pass away quietly | *friedlich sterben* |
| not suffer a painful end | *nicht leiden müssen* |
| be getting past it | *für etwas zu alt sein* |
| lose one's memory | *sein Gedächtnis verlieren* |
| be buried / cremated | *begraben / eingeäschert werden* |
| He's pushing up the daisies. | *Er schaut sich die Radieschen von unten an.* |
| She's no longer with us. | *Sie ist nicht mehr unter uns.* |
| She has left this world. | *Sie ist von uns gegangen.* |

## QUICK CHECK 10: Idioms overheard

Arthur, the prodigal son, arrives back in Nottingham. He's been away for fifteen years. Arthur (**A**), Cliff (**C**), his father's next door neighbour:

**A:** I tried to phone him but I couldn't get it organised. I didn't know what had happened.

**C:** He (*starb friedlich*) while watching the TV. He didn't (*leiden müssen*).

**A:** How was he towards the end?

**C:** Always positive. It's true he was a bit (*wacklig auf den Füßen*), but he never complained. And he *was getting* (*alt*), after all he was almost eighty.

1

## QUICK CHECK 11: Odd man out

1.

A. get long in the tooth
B. be as old as the hills
C. be at a difficult age
D. come of age

2.

A. kick the bucket
B. push up the daisies
C. sow one's wild oats
D. pass away quietly

3.

A. put someone out to pasture
B. soft-soap someone
C. lick someone's boots
D. toady to someone

### TIME FOR A SMILE

Dolly asked Priscilla why she had given up her boyfriend and she said: "I saw him diving at the swimming pool one day, and he looked different without his wallet."

## Bird's eye view

### Level 1

1. *Probleme äußerlich* – External problems
2. *Probleme innerlich* – Internal problems
3. *Ein Fall für den Spezialisten* – A case for the specialist
4. *Beim Apotheker* – At the chemist's

### Level 2

1. In the best of health – *Bei bester Gesundheit*
2. It could be better – *Könnte besser gehen*
3. Physical handicaps – *Körperliche Gebrechen*
4. Dead on one's feet – *Stehend kaputt*
5. One foot in the grave – *Mit einem Bein im Grab*

### Time for a smile

A seventy-five year old industrialist to his doctor:
"Doc, I'm getting married to a 26 year-old girl next week. Is there any advice you can give me?"
"Of course there is," said the doctor. "At your age it is dangerous to have sex. I'll give you some tablets. Take two of these every time you want to have sex." – "Before or after?" asked the old man.
"Nonsense! Instead!" replied the doctor.

# 2 LEVEL 1

The subject we probably talk most about is our health. It's often mentioned when we are small-talking at work or in private. Most idioms on health are concerned with failing or bad health. This seems to worry us most. We obviously take pleasure in telling everyone how sick, tired or even close to death we feel most of the time.

## 1. *Probleme äußerlich* – External problems

| | |
|---|---|
| *sich gründlich untersuchen lassen* | I think I need to have a thorough check-up. |
| *unter einem Sonnenstich leiden* | I'm suffering from sunstroke. What shall I do, doctor? |
| *eine hässliche Wunde* | Where did you get that nasty wound on your arm? – In a fight. |
| *verwundet werden* | I've still got pain in my leg. I was wounded in the war. |
| *verletzen; Verletzung* | He was injured in an accident and died of his injuries. |
| *Blut; bluten* | His arm was bleeding. The blood was running down his arm. |
| *verbinden; Verband* | The nurse bandaged his bleeding arm. She put a bandage round his arm. |
| *Creme gegen Sonnenbrand* | That's bad sunburn you've got there. Rub this lotion in. |

### QUICK CHECK 1: Find the noun

| | |
|---|---|
| be badly *wounded* | get a bad __________ |
| be *injured* | have an __________ |
| be *bleeding* | __________ is running down |
| *bandage* a wound | put on a __________ |

## 2. *Probleme innerlich* – Internal problems

| | |
|---|---|
| *die Zunge zeigen* | Show me your tongue. I think you've got stomach problems. |
| *nichts Ernstes* | It's nothing serious, but you'd better keep out of the sun. |
| *hoher (niederer) Blutdruck* | You've got high (low) blood pressure. |
| *überarbeitet sein* | You seem to be overworked. You should take it easier. |
| *auf seine Gesundheit achten* | You should take care of your health. Your pulse rate is too high. |
| *Cholesterinspiegel* | You should go on a diet. Your cholesterol level is too high. |
| *bei guter Gesundheit* | Mother and child are in good health. |
| *in schlechter Verfassung* | Tina is in good health. Tom, however, is in poor health. |
| *sich erkälten* | You caught a cold because you didn't put on your pullover. |
| *Grippe haben* | I've got a cold and a headache. I think I've caught the flu. |
| *wehtun* | I'll give you an injection. Don't be afraid. It won't hurt. |
| *sich erbrechen* | I've been sick three times so far. – What have you eaten? |
| *mir ist übel* | Please show me the way to the bathroom. I feel sick. |
| *eine harmlose Krankheit* | Compared with aids, flu is a harmless disease. |
| *seiner Gesundheit schaden* | Smoking can damage your health. You'd better stop smoking. |
| *zu Kräften kommen* | He's recovering his strength. He feels much better already. |
| *ansteckend; Ansteckungsgefahr* | Is this disease contagious? – No, there's no risk of infection. |
| *schmerzhafte Behandlung* | The treatment of his deep wound was very painful. |

| | |
|---|---|
| *sich den Magen verderben* | I'm feeling sick. I've got an upset stomach. |
| *in Ohnmacht fallen* | When she saw all the blood she fainted (she passed out). |
| *Es bekommt mir nicht.* | My stomach's upset. Strong coffee doesn't agree with me. |
| *Nervenzusammenbruch* | After her daughter's death she had a nervous breakdown. |
| *sich bessern* | During my holiday my health improved a lot. |
| *leiden unter* | Tina often suffers from headaches. |
| *beruhigen* | The girl saw the blood and began to cry. I tried to calm her down. |
| *Erste Hilfe* | Everybody should do a course in first aid. |
| *Linderung, Erleichterung* | These tablets will give you relief. |

## QUICK CHECK 2: Health in figures

**What does the doctor call these measurements?**

| | |
|---|---|
| number of heartbeat | ............................... |
| blood and fat | ............................... |
| arteries and pressure | ............................... |

## QUICK CHECK 3: Find just the right verb

| | |
|---|---|
| *go* | on a diet |
| ...................... | a cold |
| ...................... | one's health |
| ...................... | someone an injection |
| ...................... | one's strength |
| ...................... | from headaches |
| ...................... | someone relief |

## 3. *Ein Fall für den Spezialisten* – A case for the specialist

| | |
|---|---|
| *einen Spezialisten aufsuchen* | If I were you I would see a specialist. |
| *im Krankenhaus bleiben* | Tom is seriously ill. He must stay in hospital. |
| *ins Krankenhaus bringen* | After the crash Bill was taken to hospital. |
| *einen Herzinfarkt erleiden* | I had/suffered a heart attack last year. |
| *auf der Intensivstation liegen* | Your son is in intensive care. |
| *operiert werden* | She must be operated on. It's a matter of life and death. |
| *Chirurg* | The surgeon gave me an injection to calm me down. |
| *Schlaganfall* | Since his third stroke he has been handicapped. |
| *Frauenarzt* | Can you recommend a good gynaecologist? |
| *schwanger sein* | I'm two months pregnant. I've been feeling sick for five days. |
| *die Pille nehmen* | How long have you been on the pill? |
| *Ohrenschmerzen* | You've got earache? Go to an ear, nose and throat specialist. |

### QUICK CHECK 4: Which doctor do you go to if ...

**1.** ... you are pregnant?
**2.** ... you have a stomach ulcer?
**3.** ... you've had a cough for weeks?

### QUICK CHECK 5: Correct the typical German mistakes

**1.** Tom was brought to hospital.
**2.** He is in the intensive care.
**3.** He will be operated tomorrow.

## 4. *Beim Apotheker* – At the chemist's

| | |
|---|---|
| *die nächste Apotheke* | Where is the nearest chemist's? |
| *ein Rezept abholen* | Can I pick up the prescription in the afternoon? |
| *Medizin besorgen für* | Could you please get this medicine for me? |
| *äußerlich anzuwenden* | This lotion is for external use only. |
| *Medikament abholen* | I have to order this medicine. – When can I collect it? |
| *auf nüchternen Magen* | Take this medicine before meals, on an empty stomach. |
| *privat versichert* | I'm privately insured. (I've got private insurance.) |
| *Quittung für die Krankenkasse* | Can I have a receipt for my health insurance? |
| *gute Besserung* | I wish you a speedy recovery. |

### QUICK CHECK 6: Correct the typical German mistakes

1. Where is the next chemist?
2. For these pills you need a recipe from your doctor.
3. I wish you a fast recovery.

### TIME FOR A SMILE

A doctor is talking to a car mechanic, "Your fee is several times more per hour then we get paid for medical care."
"Yeah, but you see, doc, you always have the same model, it hasn't changed since Adam; but we have to keep up to date with new models coming every month."

**LEVEL** (m)



Ron and Anita discuss her holiday:

**R:** You're really *in the pink* after your holiday in Portugal. That sun did you good.

**A:** Thanks, but it wasn't the sun actually. It was the strong wind. I really got sun-burned. It made me sick. I had to *spew up*.

**R:** My God! I must say, now you mention it I can see a *few bags under your eyes.*

**A:** Yes, but that's probably because I've been having problems with my children. They shriek all the time. I *can't sleep a wink*. And I *feel burned out.*

**R:** Well, that's fine after your holiday.

**A:** And I think I'm pregnant!

**R:** Well, bugger me! That's the *final nail in the coffin.*

## 1. In the best of health – *Bei bester Gesundheit*

| | |
|---|---|
| be as right as rain | *in bester Verfassung sein* |
| be in fine feather | *bei bester Laune / in Hochform sein* |
| be in the pink | *bei bester Gesundheit / kerngesund sein* |
| look a picture of health | *wie das blühende Leben aussehen* |
| be as fit as a fiddle | *fit wie ein Turnschuh sein* |
| be fighting fit | *kerngesund sein* |
| feel up to the mark | *sich auf dem Posten fühlen* |
| feel in good shape | *rüstig / gut beieinander sein* |
| be in the best of health | *bei bester Gesundheit sein* |
| be as strong as a horse / an ox | *Bärenkräfte haben; bullenstark sein* |
| be as tough as old leather / old boots | *zäh wie Leder sein* |
| feel up to something | *sich einer Sache gewachsen fühlen* |
| shake off (an illness) | *(eine Krankheit) loswerden / drüber wegkommen* |
| be alive and kicking | *gesund und munter sein* |
| be fit and trim | *fit und gut durchtrainiert sein* |

2

| | |
|---|---|
| feel like a million dollars | *sich bestens fühlen* |
| be in the prime of life | *in der Blüte seines Lebens stehen* |
| take a turn for the better | *eine Wende zum Besseren nehmen* |
| feel like a new man | *sich wie neugeboren fühlen* |

### QUICK CHECK 7: Idioms overheard

Pat and Sue talk about holidays:

**P:** How was your trip to Italy? I must say (*du siehst wie das blühende Leben aus*).

**S:** It was great. Warm weather and healthy, light food. I was a bit sick before I went, but (*ich bin drüber weggekommen*) after two or three days. Now I'm (*ich fühle mich bestens*).

**P:** I'm off on holiday next week, too. I hope it'll get me back into shape. Actually I feel a bit under par at the minute.

## 2. It could be better – *Könnte besser gehen*

| | |
|---|---|
| go / be / feel under par | *nicht ganz auf der Höhe sein* |
| come down with flu | *eine Grippe kriegen* |
| feel run down | *sich ausgelaugt fühlen; erschöpft sein* |
| be down with (an illness) | *mit einer Krankheit auf der Nase liegen* |
| feel / be as sick as a dog / parrot | *sich hundsmiserabel / hundeelend fühlen* |
| be / feel under the weather | *nicht ganz auf dem Posten sein; sich unpässlich fühlen* |
| burn the candle at both ends | *sich (gesundheitlich) übernehmen; sich zu viel zumuten* |
| feel one degree under | *einen schlechten Tag haben; sich nicht so gut fühlen* |
| feel out of sorts | *sich unpässlich fühlen; nicht auf dem Damm sein* |
| feel queer | *sich komisch fühlen* |
| I have pins and needles in my legs. | *Ich habe ein Kribbeln in den Beinen.* |

| | |
|---|---|
| My legs have gone to sleep. | *Meine Beine sind mir eingeschlafen.* |
| My head is spinning. | *Mir dreht sich alles im Kopf.* |
| I feel giddy. | *Mir ist schwindelig.* |
| have bags under one's eyes | *Ringe unter den Augen haben* |
| take / catch cold | *eine Erkältung bekommen* |
| catch one's death | *sich den Tod holen* |
| puke / throw / spew up | *kotzen; sich übergeben* |
| be bed-ridden | *ans Bett gefesselt sein* |
| be out of the woods | *über den Berg sein* |
| be on one's last legs | *auf dem letzten Loch pfeifen* |
| be / feel out of shape | *nicht in Form sein* |
| feel pale / blue / green around the gills | *sich schwach / matt fühlen* |
| run a fever | *Fieber haben* |
| go under the knife | *unters Messer kommen* |
| pass out | *ohnmächtig werden* |
| patch someone up | *jemanden wieder zusammenflicken* |
| be out of breath | *außer Atem sein* |
| recharge one's batteries | *sich erholen; auftanken* |

## QUICK CHECK 8: Complete the phrases

At the doctor's, doctor and Bob:

**B:** Doctor, I *feel* completely *run-*................ . And sometimes it gets so bad I even *feel* ................ . My *head starts to* ................ .

**D:** Now calm down, Mr Kleinstück. It's all no problem. You'*ve been burning the* ............... *at both* ................ . That's why you *feel out of* ................ .

**B:** Doctor, are you sure you're right? Give me some ideas how I can ................ *my batteries.*

## 3. Physical handicaps – *Körperliche Gebrechen*

| | |
|---|---|
| be as blind as a bat | *blind sein wie ein Maulwurf* |
| be as deaf as a post | *stocktaub sein* |
| be as thin as a rake | *dünn wie eine Zaunlatte sein* |
| be as dead as a doornail | *mausetot sein* |
| be as fat as fuck (sl) | *fett wie eine Sau sein* |
| be as bald as a coot | *völlig kahl sein* |
| be as soft as a baby's bottom | *zart wie ein Babypopo sein* |

## 4. Dead on one's feet – *Stehend kaputt*

| | |
|---|---|
| go to bed with the chickens | *mit den Hühnern zu Bett gehen* |
| hit the sack / hay | *sich aufs Ohr hauen; in die Falle gehen* |
| catch / grab / have / take forty winks | *ein kurzes Nickerchen machen* |
| not sleep a wink | *kein Auge zumachen; sich schlaflose Nächte machen* |
| drop off to sleep | *einnicken; einschlafen* |
| have a kip / get some kip | *ein Schläfchen machen / pennen* |
| catch some Zs | *etwas schlafen; ein Nickerchen machen* |
| be dead beat | *wie gerädert sein; völlig kaputt sein; stehend k. o. sein* |
| be dead on one's feet | *vollkommen am Ende sein; kaum noch kriechen können* |
| conk out (sl) | *ohnmächtig werden; umkippen* |
| nod off | *einnicken* |
| be dead to the world | *bewusstlos sein; volltrunken sein* |
| sack out | *sich hinlegen; schlafen* |
| be all in | *total erschöpft sein* |
| be all tuckered out | *völlig erschöpft sein* |
| have been through the mill | *viel durchgemacht haben* |
| be more dead than alive | *mehr tot als lebendig sein* |
| be played / pooped out | *müde und matt sein* |
| feel washed out | *sich müde / ausgelaugt fühlen* |
| wear someone out | *jemanden auslaugen* |
| Show a leg! | *Aufstehen! Raus aus den Federn!* |

## QUICK CHECK 9: Can you speed-read this?

We've replaced the vowels with *x*s.

Ron complains to Anne:

**R:** I didn't *slxxp x wxnk* last night. I was lying awake thinking about the business.

**A:** I must say you *lxxk xll txckxrxd xxt.* Listen, you *grxb fxxrty wxnks* and I'll finish off this chapter.

**R:** I think I need more than forty winks. I think I'll take a week off before I *cxnk xxt* completely. Is that okay with you?

## 5. One foot in the grave – *Mit einem Bein im Grab*

| | |
|---|---|
| drop dead in one's tracks | *mitten im Leben / in der Arbeit zusammenbrechen* |
| come within an inch of losing one's life | *jemandes Leben hängt an einem seidenen Faden* |
| look like death warmed up | *aussehen wie eine Leiche auf Urlaub* |
| catch one's death of cold | *sich den Tod holen* |
| be the final nail in the coffin | *der letzte Nagel zum Sarg sein* |
| have one foot in the grave | *mit einem Bein im Grabe stehen* |
| be at death's door | *dem Tode ganz nah sein* |
| give up the ghost | *den Geist aufgeben* |
| be as dead as a dodo / doornail | *mausetot sein* |
| push up (the) daisies | *sich die Radieschen von unten angucken* |
| be a goner | *erledigt sein; ein Todeskandidat sein* |
| not be long for this world | *nicht mehr lange zu leben haben* |
| It's curtains for you. | *Für dich ist die Sache gelaufen.* |
| breathe one's last (breath) | *seinen letzten Atemzug tun* |
| cash in one's chips | *den Löffel abgeben* |
| die a natural death | *eines natürlichen Todes sterben* |
| die in one's boots | *in den Stiefeln sterben; plötzlich und unerwartet sterben* |
| kick off; kick the bucket | *den Löffel abgeben* |
| meet one's end | *sterben* |
| pass away / on | *aus dem Leben scheiden* |

## QUICK CHECK 10: Find the mistakes

Doctor and nurse in a hospital:

**D:** Quick nurse, pass me the oxygen. This patient is *within a millimeter of loosing his life.*

**N:** He does look bad. We thought he was going to be all right, but that pneumonia *was the final screw in his coffin.*

**D:** Never mind! If we don't act quickly he *won't be long for this earth.* Let's do our best.

### TIME FOR A SMILE

The patient shook his doctor's hand in gratitude and said, "Since we are the best of friends, I would not want to insult you by offering payment. But I would like you to know that I have mentioned you in my will."
"That is very kind of you," said the doctor emotionally, and then added, "Can I see that prescription I just gave you? I'd like to make a little change."

## Bird's eye view

### Level I

1. *Den Tisch reservieren* – Booking the table
2. *Tischgespräche* – Table talk
3. *Gespräch mit dem Ober* – Talking to the waiter
4. *Sonderwünsche* – Special needs
5. *Ein Lob für den Koch* – Praising the cook
6. *Sich beschweren* – Making a complaint
7. *Die Rechnung, bitte* – The bill, please

### Level II

1. Toasting – *Zuprosten*
2. Ways of drinking – *Wie man trinkt*
3. The way we eat – *Wie wir essen*
4. Good night – *Gute Nacht*

### Time for a smile

An elderly couple were killed in an accident and found themselves being given a tour of heaven by Saint Peter. "Here is your oceanside cottage, over there are the tennis courts, swimming pool, and two golf courses. If you need any refreshments, just stop by any of the many bars located throughout the area."

"Heck, Gloria," the old man hissed when Saint Peter had walked off, "we could have been here ten years ago if you hadn't heard about all those stupid low-fat diets!"

## LEVEL 1

It's easy to book a table by phone. Sometimes, however, there are misunderstandings when you want to know about the local cuisine – in this case you have to be very specific. No general questions. You can ask, for example, which red wines fit best with the venison. Of course, this only works with quality restaurants.

### 1. *Den Tisch reservieren* – Booking the table

| | |
|---|---|
| *Arbeitsessen* | What about a working lunch? |
| *zu einem Abendessen einladen* | Can I invite you out tonight? |
| *zu einem guten Abendessen einladen* | May I wine and dine you? |
| *einfach und billig* | There's a simple and inexpensive restaurant around here. |
| *regionale Spezialitäten* | They do good local meals there. |
| *heimische Küche* | They do / serve very good local cuisine. |
| *einen Tisch reservieren* | Have you reserved / booked a table? |
| *Nichtraucherbereich* | Could I please have / book a table in the non-smoking area? |
| *in der Ecke, am Fenster* | Would you like a table in the corner or by the window? |
| *auf welchen Namen* | What name is it, please? |
| *ausgebucht* | Sorry, we're full this evening. |

### QUICK CHECK 1: Tim, the yes-man

Tim echos Tom, but he uses different phrases:

**Tom:** What would you advise me? Shall I *take Tina out* tonight?
**Tim:** Yes, Tom, if I were you I'd ....................
**Tom:** What about the Red Lion? They do good *local meals* there.
**Tim:** Yes, they do very good ....................
**Tom:** Should I *reserve* a table?
**Tim:** Yes, if I were you I'*d* ...............a table.

## 2. *Tischgespräche* – Table talk

| | |
|---|---|
| *Was essen / trinken Sie?* | What will you have? |
| *Schweine- oder Kalbfleisch?* | Do you prefer pork or veal? |
| *Muscheln mögen* | Do you like mussels? |
| *sich nicht viel machen aus* | I don't care much for seafood. |
| *Spezialität des Hauses* | I always have the chef's special. |
| *am liebsten essen* | What kind of fish do you like best? |
| *empfehlen* | What would you recommend? |
| *Weine aus der Gegend* | They serve very good wines from this region. |
| *empfehlenswerte Gerichte / Speisen* | There are several dishes worth eating here. |
| *Sie machen sehr gute regionale Fleischgerichte.* | They do very good local meat dishes. |
| *ausgezeichnete Schweinshaxe bekommen* | You can get excellent pork knuckle. |
| *Wild schmeckt am besten.* | The tastiest thing here in my opinion is the game. |
| *Das Reh ist hier sehr gut.* | They serve very good venison. |

### QUICK CHECK 2: Understanding the menu

What is it?

| | |
|---|---|
| **1.** The meet of an ox | beef |
| **2.** The meat of a pig | ........................................ |
| **3.** The meat of a baby cow | ........................................ |
| **4.** The meat of a deer | ........................................ |
| **5.** Mussels or lobster | ........................................ |

### TIME FOR A SMILE

***VIPs on food***

I just love Chinese food. My favourite dish is 127. *Clement Atlee*

I will not eat oysters. I want my food dead. Not sick, not wounded, dead. *Woody Allen*

McDonald's in Tokyo is a terrible revenge for Pearl Harbour. *S. I. Hayakawa*

3

## 3. *Gespräch mit dem Ober* – Talking to the waiter

| | |
|---|---|
| *Speisenkarte und Weinkarte* | Could I have the menu and the wine list, please? |
| *wählen, bestellen* | Are you ready to order? |
| *Ich habe mich noch nicht entschieden.* | Sorry. I haven't decided yet. |
| *Bestellung aufnehmen* | Waiter! Could you take my order? I've got a train to catch. |
| *Was sind Ihre Spezialitäten?* | What are your specialities? |
| *Gibt es heute etwas Besonderes?* | Is there anything special today? |
| *Tagesgericht* | What's today's special? |
| *die Spezialität des Kochs* | What's the chef's special? |
| *anfangen mit* | What would you like to start with? |
| *Das nehme ich.* | I've never eaten wild boar. That'll be my choice. |
| *Und ich nehme die Ente.* | And I'll take the duck. |
| *versuchen* | I'll try the lamb. |
| *nehmen* | I'll have the pork chop. |
| *Ich hätte gern die Suppe und danach ein Steak.* | I'll have the soup and a steak to follow, please. |
| *Wie hätten Sie das Steak gern?* | How would you like the steak? |
| *Englisch (blutig) / medium / durchgebraten.* | Rare / medium / well done. |
| *Und als Gemüse / Beilage?* | And the vegetables? |
| *ein kleiner Salat* | Just a side salad, please. |
| *Und danach?* | And to follow? |
| *beim Rotwein bleiben* | I suggest we stay with red wine. |
| *eine halbe Flasche* | I'll have a half bottle of the Chablis, please. |
| *ein großes Dunkles* | a pint of bitter |
| *ein kleines Helles* | a half of lager |
| *Schmeckt Ihnen der Wein?* | Is the wine to your liking? |
| *schmecken* | Did you enjoy your meal? – Oh yes, it was excellent. |
| *Würden Sie mir bitte den Senf geben?* | Would you mind passing the mustard, please? |
| *noch ein bisschen* | Would you like some more soup? – No thanks, I'm full. |

| | |
|---|---|
| *das Dessert bestellen* | Could we order the sweet / dessert now? |
| *Diese Runde geht auf mich. Was möchten Sie?* | This round's on me. What are you having? |
| *Danke, keinen Alkohol für mich, bitte. Ich muss noch fahren.* | No alcohol for me, thanks. I'm driving. |
| *Zum Wohl! / Prost!* | Your health! / Cheers! |
| *Dürfen wir um Ihre letzten Bestellungen bitten!* | Last orders. Please! |
| *Es ist Zeit, wir schließen gleich.* | Time, Ladies and Gentlemen, please. |

## QUICK CHECK 3: What to say to the waiter

You want ...

| | |
|---|---|
| **1.** the list with the meals: | Could ...................., please? |
| **2.** to choose the wine: | Could ...................., please? |
| **3.** to tell the waiter your choice: | Could ...................., please? |

## QUICK CHECK 4: Find the chronological order

Put the correct number into the boxes.

- ❑ Last orders. Please!
- ❑ I'm full.
- ❑ And the vegetables?
- ❑ Time, Ladies and Gentlemen, please.
- ❑ And to follow?

### TIME FOR A SMILE

A customer was bothering the waiter. First, he asked that the air conditioning be turned up because he was too hot, then he asked it be turned down because he was too cold, and so on for about half an hour. Surprisingly, the waiter was very patient, he walked back and forth and never once got angry. Finally, a second customer asked him why he didn't throw the pest out.
"Oh, I really don't care," said the waiter with a smile. "We don't even have an air conditioner."

3

## 4. *Sonderwünsche* – Special needs

| | |
|---|---|
| *etwas sofort haben* | We're in a bit of a hurry. What can we have without waiting? |
| *ein zweiter Löffel* | Could I have a second spoon, please? |
| *statt des Nachtischs* | Could I have an orange instead of the dessert? |
| *Kinderportion* | Do you also serve children's portions? |
| *Diätkost anbieten* | Do you offer dietary food, as well? I'm a diabetic. |
| *noch eine Portion* | I'd like a second helping. |
| *vegetarische Kost* | Do you have vegetarian food? |
| *vegetarische Gerichte* | Could you recommend me a vegetarian dish? |
| *cholesterinarme Gerichte* | Do you have low-cholesterol dishes? I'm on a diet, you know. |
| *kalorienarm* | Do you serve any low-fat dishes? |
| *koffeinfreier Kaffee* | Decaffeinated coffee for my mother, please. |

### QUICK CHECK 5: Is it true or false?

| | True | False |
|---|---|---|
| **1.** The sweet is the dessert. | | |
| **2.** Venison is a green salad. | | |
| **3.** Wild boar is a vegetarian dish. | | |
| **4.** The menu is made of paper. | | |
| **5.** Low-cholesterol dishes are low-fat dishes. | | |
| **6.** A second helping is the same as a second spoon. | | |

### TIME FOR A SMILE

"Waiter! Waiter! What is this fly doing in my soup?"
"Hm ... breaststroke, I think."

## 5. *Ein Lob für den Koch* – Praising the cook

| | |
|---|---|
| *Auf ein so gutes Abendessen war ich nicht gefasst.* | I hadn't expected such a good dinner. |
| *Das war wirklich ausgezeichnet.* | That was really excellent. |
| *Sie müssen mir das Rezept geben.* | You must let me have the recipe. |
| *Ich muss wirklich sagen, du verstehst zu leben.* | I must say you certainly know what's what. |
| *Das ist einmalig!* | That's second to none! |
| *Das ist absolute Spitze!* | It's out of this world! |
| *Das ist meisterhaft!* | That's a touch of perfection! |
| *Das Essen war hervorragend.* | The food was second to none. |

## 6. *Sich beschweren* – Making a complaint

| | |
|---|---|
| *ich warte immer noch auf* | Excuse me! I'm still waiting for my steak. |
| *lange dauern* | We have been waiting for 20 minutes. What's taking so long? |
| *dauert es noch lange?* | Excuse me, will it be much longer before we're served? |
| *nicht bestellt haben* | Fish?! But that is not what I ordered. I asked for chicken. |
| *nicht gar* | It isn't properly cooked. |
| *verkocht* | I'm sorry but this is overcooked. |
| *medium; roh* | I asked for it medium but this is almost rare. |
| *zu stark durchgebraten* | Waiter! I'm afraid this steak is overdone. |
| *Irrtum* | That's not what I wanted. There must be some mistake. |
| *nicht durchgebraten* | Waiter! I wanted my steak well done, this one is underdone. |
| *den Geschäftsführer sprechen* | Waiter! I'd like to see the manager. |
| *sich beschweren über* | Are you the manager? I'd like to complain about the food. |
| *nicht akzeptieren* | There are some things here that I really can't accept. |

3

## QUICK CHECK 6: The chef's mistakes

How should your dish be done? Tick off the correct method.

1. Waiter, I told you I can't stand any blood. I wanted my steak
   **A.** overdone **B.** well-done **C.** rare
2. Waiter, should green beans be
   **A.** raw **B.** over-boiled **C.** well-cooked
3. Waiter, why don't you serve the potatoes
   **A.** boiled **B.** stewed **C.** raw?

## 7. *Die Rechnung, bitte* – The bill, please

| | |
|---|---|
| *Zahlen, bitte!* | Could you let me have the bill, please? |
| *Bitte zahlen.* | Waiter! Can I have the bill, please? |
| *zusammen oder getrennt?* | Separate bills? – No, all on my bill, please. |
| *getrennte Rechnung* | Separate bills, please. |
| *getrennt bezahlen* | We'd like to pay separately. Do you take credit cards? |
| *Das übernehme ich.* | Let me get this. |
| *Sie sind unser Gast.* | No, no! This is on us! |
| *Das geht auf meine Rechnung.* | It's my treat. |
| *Wie viel Trinkgeld gibt man?* | How much do you normally tip the waitress? |
| *Nehmen Sie Schecks?* | Do you accept cheques? |
| *Nehmen Sie Kreditkarten?* | Do you take credit cards? |
| *Mit der Rechnung stimmt etwas nicht.* | I think there's something wrong with the bill. |
| *Beleg* | Could I have a receipt, please? |
| *Stimmt so.* | Keep the change. |
| *Service inbegriffen* | Is the service included? |
| *Betrag* | What's this amount for? We didn't have any dessert. |
| *Fehler in der Rechnung* | Waitress! I'm afraid there's a mistake in the bill. |

## LEVEL 3

Ron meets Bob on the street:

**B:** My God, Ron. You've been *painting the town red*, haven't you?
**R:** What do you mean? I'm *as sober as a judge.*
**B:** You don't seem to be. I thought you'd *turned over a new leaf.*
**R:** Well, I had to fire somebody. Oh, I've got *a bit of a sweet tooth.* Have you got any chocolate in your pocket?
**B:** Chocolate? You should go home to bed. You should *sleep it off.*

### 1. Toasting – *Zuprosten*

| | |
|---|---|
| Cheers! | *Prost* |
| To your good health! | *Auf Ihr Wohl!* |
| I'd like to propose a toast to the conclusion of our contract. | *Ich schlage vor, wir trinken auf den Abschluss unseres Vertrags.* |
| Let's raise our glasses to the future of Europe. | *Erheben wir unsere Gläser und trinken wir auf die Zukunft Europas.* |
| I rise to toast our guests. | *Ich erhebe mich, um auf das Wohl unserer Gäste zu trinken.* |
| I'd like to make a toast to our new colleague. | *Ich möchte einen Toast auf unseren neuen Kollegen ausbringen.* |
| Ladies and Gentlemen, let's celebrate this with a glass of champagne. | *Meine Damen und Herren, begießen wir es mit einem Glas Champagner.* |
| Here's to the beautiful bride! | *Auf das Wohl der schönen Braut!* |
| I want to wish the newly wed couple all the best. | *Ich wünsche dem neu vermählten Paar alles Gute.* |
| Best of luck, you two. And now everybody, bottoms up! | *Viel Glück euch beiden. Und nun hoch die Tassen!* |

**TIME FOR A SMILE**

"Waiter! You've brought me a lobster with only one claw."
"I'm ever so sorry, sir, but it lost its claw in a fight."
"Never mind! Take it away and bring me the winner."

## QUICK CHECK 7: Beautiful people

Can you repair the words?

Ah, here comes the beautiful bride.
Everybody, *let's bracelete* her beauty with a glass of champagne.
*To here is* the charming bride.
And I also want to *wish* you and Steve *the ulck of steb* in your new life over in Germany.

### TIME FOR A SMILE

A tourist saw an advertisement for a restaurant which claimed that any dish requested could be served. The man decided to test this restaurant. He entered and ordered an elephant on toast. The waiter took the order and went away into the kitchen. A few minutes later, he returned and said calmly, "We do apologise, sir, but we have run out of bread."

## 2. Ways of drinking – *Wie man trinkt*

| | |
|---|---|
| be / go on the wagon | *keinen Tropfen mehr trinken* |
| be as sober as a judge; be stone-cold sober | *stocknüchtern sein* |
| drink in sips | *in kleinen Schlucken trinken* |
| wet one's whistle | *sich die Kehle anfeuchten; sich einen genehmigen* |
| drink one's fill | *einen anständigen Schluck nehmen; sich einen genehmigen* |
| have a drop too much | *einen über den Durst trinken; zu tief ins Glas schauen* |
| take to drink | *zur Flasche greifen* |
| drink like a fish | *wie ein Loch saufen* |
| paint the town red | *auf Zechtour gehen* |
| spend a night on the tiles | *die ganze Nacht durchzechen* |
| go on a binge; go on a pub crawl | *auf Sauftour gehen* |
| hit the bottle | *anfangen zu saufen; sich dem Suff hingeben* |

| | |
|---|---|
| Dutch courage | *angetrunkener Mut* |
| be as drunk as a lord | *voll wie ein Strandhaubitze sein* |
| be as drunk as a skunk (US); be pissed as a newt (sl); be pissed out of one's mind (sl) | *blau wie ein Veilchen sein* |
| take a hair of the dog that bit one | *den Kater mit Schnaps vertreiben; mit dem anfangen, mit dem man aufgehört hat* |
| turn over a new leaf | *sich zum Besseren ändern; einen neuen Anfang machen* |
| have a hangover | *einen Kater haben* |

## QUICK CHECK 8: You'd better go on the wagon

Annette and Ron discuss his problems:

**A:** *Why have you ......................... to drink* again? What's happened?
**R:** I ....................... *the bottle* after we got the company results. Yesterday *I* ......................... *the town red.* And now I've *got a* ......................... .
**A:** Well, I'm not surprised. It serves you right.

### TIME FOR A SMILE

Grandpa was celebrating his 100th birthday and everybody complimented him on how well-preserved he appeared. "Gentlemen, I will tell you the secret of my success," he cackled. "I have been in the open air day after day for some 75 years now."
The celebrants were impressed and asked how he had managed to keep up his fitness regime. "Well, you see, my wife and I were married 75 years ago. On our wedding night, we made a solemn pledge. Whenever we had a fight, the one who was proved wrong would go outside and take a walk."

## 3. The way we eat – *Wie wir essen*

| | |
|---|---|
| eat out | *essen gehen* |
| It makes my mouth water. | *Mir läuft das Wasser im Mund zusammen.* |
| eat to one's heart's content | *nach Herzenslust essen* |
| have a sweet tooth | *eine Schwäche für Süßes haben* |
| It'll stick to your ribs. | *Das wird ein Weilchen vorhalten.* |
| grab / have a bite | *etwas essen; einen Bissen zu sich nehmen* |
| pick at one's food | *in seinem Essen herumstochern; nicht hungrig sein* |
| scoff / wolf something down | *etwas gierig verschlingen* |
| put away food / drink | *Essen verdrücken / Getränke runterkippen* |
| eat one's fill | *sich satt essen* |
| I could eat a horse. | *Ich könnte ein Pferd verschlingen.* |
| cram something down one's throat | *etwas in sich hineinstopfen* |
| eat one's head off | *fressen wie ein Scheunendrescher; für zwei essen* |
| I could murder a meal / a beer. | *Ich könnte jetzt ein Essen / ein Bier verdrücken.* |
| eat someone out of house and home | *jemandem die Haare vom Kopf fressen* |
| put on weight | *Gewicht zulegen; schwerer werden* |
| go Dutch | *getrennte Rechnung machen* |
| pick up the tab; foot the bill | *für die Kosten aufkommen; die Zeche zahlen* |

## QUICK CHECK 9: Get the idioms right

After the jog. Bob and Sue:

**B:** That was twenty kilometres. But now I could *murder a weight.*

**S:** Wait a minute! Think of the *steak you'll cram on.* The jog will be wasted.

**B:** Well, look at all the food you *put down your throat* and you never put any weight on.

**S:** No, but you do!

TIME FOR A SMILE

***Stupid labels on food packages and tins***

On a bag of Fritos: You could be a winner! No purchase necessary. Details inside.
On Marks & Spencer bread pudding: Product will be hot after heating.

## QUICK CHECK 10: Body idioms

Put these words where they belong.

| | | |
|---|---|---|
| mouth | content | rib |
| head | water | sweet |
| tooth | stick | heart |

**1.** The delicious smell from the kitchen made my ....................... .
**2.** And I could eat caviar and oysters to my ............................. .
**3.** There was a T-bone steak that would ..................to my ............... .
**4.** Anne knew that I have a ..................... The desert was second to none.
**5.** I hope you aren't going to eat her ........................ off.

## 4. Good night – *Gute Nacht*

| | |
|---|---|
| have a good night's sleep | *sich richtig ausschlafen* |
| not sleep a wink | *kein Auge zumachen* |
| be awake every five minutes | *immer wieder wach werden; nicht durchschlafen* |
| have forty winks | *ein kurzes Nickerchen halten* |
| hit the sack / hay | *sich aufs Ohr hauen* |
| have a kip; get some kip | *pofen; schlafen* |
| Sweet dreams! | *Schlaf schön! Träum was Süßes!* |
| get a bit of shut-eye | *ein Schläfchen machen* |
| Sleep on it! | *Schlaf erst mal drüber.* |

| | |
|---|---|
| sleep like a log / top | *wie ein Murmeltier / Klotz / Stein schlafen* |
| Show a leg! | *Aufstehen! Raus aus den Federn!* |
| Sleep it off! | *Schlaf deinen Rausch aus!* |

## QUICK CHECK 11: The choice is yours

Ron and Bob:

**R:** Hi Bob. Where's Michael from Munich?

**B:** He's *having* [**A.** *forty* **B.** *fifty* **C.** *twenty*] *winks* after his pub crawl.

**R:** It's almost lunch-time. When did he *hit the* [**A.** *bed* **B.** *sack* **C.** *grass*]?

**B:** At almost five in the morning. But he's been *sleeping like a* [**A.** *dog* **B.** *bear* **C.** *log*] ever since.

**R:** Okay, let's leave him to *sleep it* [**A.** *off* **B.** *down* **C.** *over*].

## QUICK CHECK 12: Remember the idiom?

**1.** having given up drinking alcohol, either temporarily or permanently:

........................................................................

**2.** another alcoholic drink to cure the effects of the alcohol drunk previously:

........................................................................

**3.** to have a little drink, especially an alcoholic one:

........................................................................

**4.** to eat something in a very quick and hungry way

........................................................................

### TIME FOR A SMILE

A drunk phoned police to report that thieves had been in his car. "They've stolen the dashboard, the steering wheel, the brake pedal, the radio, and even the accelerator," he cried out.
However, before the police investigation could start, the phone rang a second time and the same voice came over the line. "Never mind," he said with a hiccup, "I got in the back seat by mistake."

## Bird's eye view

### LEVEL I

1. *Der Körperbau* – The frame
2. *Die Frisur* – The hairstyle
3. *Das Gesicht* – The face
4. *Kleidung und andere Merkmale* – Clothes and other characteristics

### LEVEL II

1. Resemblance – *Ähnlichkeit*
2. Facial expression – *Gesichtsausdruck*
3. From head to toe – *Von Kopf bis Fuß*
4. Fine feathers make fine birds – *Kleider machen Leute*
5. Stages of life – *Lebensabschnitte*

### Time for a smile

"You know," said the woman to her friend as she watched her husband walking down the road, "it's becoming harder and harder to remember that he was the man who made me forget Paul Newman."

## LEVEL 1

We spend a lot of time watching each other. We do this in great detail, talking about our bodies, hairstyles, faces and clothing. And of course, when we see somebody or something new we feel we have to make comparisons with similar things from our experience. We need a whole series of phrases for that, too. So to find out how we talk about each other, read on!

### 1. *Der Körperbau* – The frame

| | |
|---|---|
| *hübsch (Frauen); hübsch (Männer)* | Women are pretty, men are handsome; both can be good-looking. |
| *gutes Aussehen* | Tom is proud of Tina's good looks. |
| *breit wie ein Kleiderschrank sein* | Tom is a big man. He is as broad as a barn. |
| *athletischer Körperbau* | Tom has an athletic build. He's as strong as an ox. |
| *zart, schwächlich* | At the age of nine he was a delicate / fragile boy. |
| *hässlich wie die Nacht* | He's as ugly as sin. |
| *zu kurz geraten* | Tim is not very tall. He's a bit on the short side. |
| *so alt sein, wie man aussieht* | Tina is 32, but she really doesn't look her age. |
| *jugendliche Erscheinung* | She looks younger than she is. She still has a youthful appearance. |
| *schick aussehen* | You look very smart. Are you going out? |
| *äußere Erscheinung* | I met Jill's friend today and was shocked by his appearance. |
| *das gewisse Etwas haben* | She has something about herself that makes her attractive. |
| *kräftig gebaut sein* | Sarah is not slightly built, she is strongly built. |
| *groß für sein Alter* | Sam is only 10 years old and already very tall for his age. |
| *unansehnlich sein* | She's rather a plain girl, but she has a good character. |
| *sich verändern* | I hardly recognized you. You have changed a lot. |
| *klein (von Statur)* | Napoleon was a short man, but a great leader. |

## QUICK CHECK 1: Complete the comparisons

1. Tom is as broad as a ................................................................ .
2. He's as strong as an ................................................................ .
3. Unfortunately, he's as ugly as ............................................... .

## QUICK CHECK 2: A question of size

1. He's a bit on the ......................... side.
2. She's already very ......................... for her age.
3. Napoleon was a ......................... man, but a ......................... leader.

## 2. *Die Frisur* – The hairstyle

| | |
|---|---|
| *Locken* | Her hair falls in natural curls over her shoulders. |
| *Naturwelle* | Tina has a natural wave in her hair. |
| *grau werden* | Tom's hair is going grey although he's only forty-five. |
| *lockiges Haar; glattes Haar* | Tina has long curly black hair; Tom has straight short hair. |
| *seine Haare färben* | Tom dyes his hair because he is going grey. |
| *sich eine Dauerwelle machen lassen* | Tina has a perm done every week. |
| *ungekämmt* | You look very untidy. Your hair is unkempt. Here is a comb. |
| *völlig kahl sein, eine Glatze haben* | Tim's hair is falling out. In a year he will be as bald as a coot. |
| *volles, dichtes Haar haben* | Tina has a fine head of hair. She wears it long and curly. |
| *helles Haar* | Tim has got fair hair, but he dyes it brown. |
| *kahl sein* | I'm losing all my hair. In a year I'll be bald. |
| *zum Friseur müssen* | I think you need a hair cut, Tom. I hate shoulder-length hair. |

## QUICK CHECK 3: What's the opposite?

| | |
|---|---|
| As a boy Tim had a fine head of hair. | Today he's as *b*______ as a coot. |
| Sue has a natural wave in her hair. | Tina gets her hair *p*_______ every two months. |
| She wears it long and curly. | Anne has got short and ____hair. |

## 3. *Das Gesicht* – The face

| | |
|---|---|
| *blass aussehen* | You're looking pale. Are you ill? – No, I always look pale. |
| *sonnengebräunt* | He came back from his holiday suntanned / bronzed. |
| *Sonnenbräune* | Fair haired or pale people will never get a good suntan. |
| *Tränensäcke unter den Augen* | Tina's looking pale today and she's got bags under her eyes. |
| *Gesichter sind rund, eckig, oval* | Tim's face is not round, it's angular. Jill has an oval face. |
| *eine reine Haut haben* | Tina has a clear complexion. So she only uses eye-shadow. |
| *glatt rasiert* | Tom hasn't got a beard. He is clean-shaven. |
| *ein ebenmäßiges Gesicht haben* | He shouldn't hide his even-featured face under a beard. |
| *blaue Augen haben* | Do you know the song "Baby's got blue eyes"? |
| *schielen* | Tim's cross-eyed. Maybe his eyes are too close together. He's got a squint. |
| *dünne Lippen* | Her mouth looks cruel because she has very thin lips. |
| *Hakennase; Himmelfahrtsnase* | Tony has a hooked nose; his wife has a nice turned-up nose. |
| *Stupsnase; spitze Nase* | Anne has a little snub nose. Andrew has a long pointed nose. |
| *ein gewinnendes Lächeln* | With her winning smile she can twist Tom round her finger. |

## QUICK CHECK 4: Describe these noses

a ........................ nose

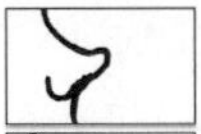
a ........................ nose

a ........................ nose

a ........................ nose

## 4. *Kleidung und andere Merkmale* – Clothes and other characteristics

| | |
|---|---|
| *sich gut kleiden* | Tina's always very elegant. She dresses so well. |
| *einen teuren Geschmack haben* | She spends Tom's salary on dresses. She has an expensive taste. |
| *mit der Mode gehen* | Tina dresses well. She's always in fashion. |
| *sich geschmacklos anziehen* | Tom wears shabby clothes. He dresses tastelessly. |
| *Kleider von der Stange* | Tom has no flair for fashion. He only buys off the peg. |
| *Maßanzüge tragen* | Ron is a rich boy. All his suits are tailor-made. |
| *ein Frauentyp sein* | He's a ladies' man / womaniser. |
| *Diät halten / auf Diät sein* | Lisa is getting thinner and thinner. She must be on a diet. |
| *die Männerblicke auf sich ziehen* | She can really pull the men the way she dresses. |

## QUICK CHECK 5: Bob and Ron are different

| | |
|---|---|
| Bob always looks pale. | *Ron has a good* ................. . |
| Bob doesn't dress *well.* | Ron is always in ...................... . |
| Bob only buys .......................... . | All Ron's suits are *tailor-made.* |
| Bob's face is .......................... . | Ron's face is *round.* |

### TIME FOR A SMILE

*Sign in a shop window*

OUR CLOTHES NOT ONLY MAKE GIRLS SLIM,
THEY ALSO MAKE MEN LOOK ROUND.

4

## LEVEL

Anita and Ortrud discuss an old colleague of theirs:

**A:** My goodness! Do you know who I met the other day. Guess!
**O:** Tut. What a waste of time! How can I guess what's in your mind?
**A:** I met Lucy. I didn't recognise here. She spoke to me and I didn't know who she was. She went *as red as a beetroot.*
**O:** Why didn't you recognise her?
**A:** Well, she used to be *a bit of hot stuff,* at least that's what all the men said. And now *she looks a sight.*
**O:** Why, what's happened?
**A:** She's got *a spare tyre,* or several, I'd say.
**O:** Well, beauty *is only skin-deep,* or so they say.

### 1. Resemblance – *Ähnlichkeit*

| | |
|---|---|
| be cast in the same mould | *aus demselben Holz geschnitzt sein* |
| It runs in the family. | *Das liegt in der Familie.* |
| as different as chalk and cheese | *so verschieden wie Tag und Nacht* |
| be the spitting image of someone | *jemandem wie aus dem Gesicht geschnitten sein* |
| She is the spit (and image) of her mother. | *Sie ist ihrer Mutter wie aus dem Gesicht geschnitten.* |
| be as like as two peas (in a pod) | *sich wie ein Ei dem anderen gleichen* |
| be a chip off the old block | *ganz der Vater sein; der Apfel fällt nicht weit vom Stamm.* |
| be a dead ringer for someone | *das Ebenbild / ein Doppelgänger von jemandem sein* |
| Birds of a feather flock together. | *Gleich und Gleich gesellt sich gern.* |
| kindred spirits | *verwandte Seelen* |
| a meeting of minds | *eine Begegnung gleicher Gesinnungen* |
| spiritual kinship | *Geistes- / Seelenverwandtschaft* |
| be soulmates | *seelenverwandt sein* |
| be tarred with the same brush | *kein Haar / keinen Deut besser sein* |
| bear no likeliness / resemblance to | *keine Ähnlichkeit haben mit; nicht ähneln* |

| | |
|---|---|
| be someone's double | *jemandes Doppelgänger sein* |
| have something in common with | *etwas mit jemandem gemeinsam haben* |
| pass as someone | *sich ausgeben für* |
| take after someone | *nach jemandem kommen, jemandem nachgeschlagen sein* |
| be two of a kind | *vom gleichen Schlag sein* |

## QUICK CHECK 6: Four mistakes to correct

Receptionist and secretary at their coffee break:

**R:** Did you see that woman who came for an interview this morning? She*'s the spitting picture of* Lucy Bruhn.

**S:** Actually, she's Lucy's younger sister. They *are as like as two pees in a pot.* And they both *make after their mother.*

**R:** Well, I hope the new girl works as hard as her sister.

### TIME FOR A SMILE

Two elderly ladies met at a banquet after an absence of ten years. Said the first, "Good gracious, Elizabeth, I haven't seen you for ages. You certainly look a lot older."
"You look much older too, Dorothy, dear. I wouldn't have recognised you except for the dress and hat."

## 2. Facial expression – *Gesichtsausdruck*

| | |
|---|---|
| go as red as a beetroot | *rot wie eine Tomate werden* |
| thumb one's nose at someone | *jemandem eine lange Nase machen* |
| turn one's nose up | *die Nase rümpfen* |
| keep a stiff upper lip | *Haltung bewahren* |
| grin all over one's face | *über das ganze Gesicht grinsen* |
| go bright red | *knallrot werden* |
| have egg on one's face | *dumm aus der Wäsche gucken* |
| look seedy | *verdächtig / zwielichtig aussehen* |
| po-faced Mr Block | *Herr Block mit seinem Pokergesicht* |

| | |
|---|---|
| pull a long face | *ein langes Gesicht machen* |
| keep a straight face | *keine Miene verziehen* |
| put on a brave face | *gute Miene zum bösen Spiel machen* |
| grin and bear it | *gute Miene zum bösen Spiel machen* |
| without flinching | *ohne eine Miene zu verziehen* |
| without batting an eyelid | *ohne mit der Wimper zu zucken* |
| raise one's eyebrows (at someone) | *die Stirn missbilligend runzeln* |
| knit one's brow | *die Stirn in Denkfalten legen* |
| cause raised eyebrows | *Aufsehen oder Missfallen erregen* |
| look down one's nose at someone | *jemanden von oben herab betrachten* |
| Wipe that stupid look off your face! | *Mach nicht so ein dummes Gesicht!* |
| make a sour face | *ein saures Gesicht machen* |
| go as white as a sheet | *blass wie ein Leichentuch werden* |
| pull a wry face | *ein schiefes Gesicht machen* |
| give someone a black / filthy look | *jemandem einen finsteren Blick zuwerfen* |
| look askance at someone | *jemanden schief / scheel anblicken* |
| If looks could kill. | *Wenn Blicke töten könnten.* |

## QUICK CHECK 7: Fill them in

Two clerks talk about the company doctor:

**P:** And the doctor asked me when I last drank wine. I couldn't *keep my face* .......................... .

**J:** What did you tell him? You drink more than a bottle every day.

**P:** I told him that. He *gave me* .......................... *look.*

**J:** Well, be careful. You could ruin your liver. Then you'll *have* ................. *on your face.*

### TIME FOR A SMILE

I can't understand the fuss over computer pornography. Surely everybody has seen a computer without clothes on by now.

## QUICK CHECK 8: Remember the idioms?

1. When the department leader read out a complaint the hot-line clerk (*wurde rot wie eine Tomate*).
2. Ron told Tom his work was not good enough. Tom wasn't interested and (*rümpfte seine Nase*) at Ron.
3. Okay, she's left you and it's difficult. Never mind, you've got to (*Haltung bewahren*) in any case.

## 3. From head to toe – *Von Kopf bis Fuß*

| | |
|---|---|
| be a bit of hot stuff | *ein steiler Zahn sein* |
| be a cracker / smasher | *ein rasanter Feger sein* |
| be a sight for sore eyes | *eine Augenweide sein* |
| be nothing but skin and bones | *nur Haut und Knochen sein* |
| cut a good / sorry figure | *eine gute / schlechte Figur abgeben* |
| Butter wouldn't melt in her mouth. | *Sie kann kein Wässerchen trüben; sie ist die Unschuld in Person.* |
| be as bald as a coot / as a billiard ball | *total kahlköpfig sein* |
| be / look green / pale / rosy about the gills | *grün / rosig / blass im Gesicht sein* |
| have a face like the back of a bus; be butt-ugly | *hässlich sein wie die Nacht schwarz* |
| be as fresh as the dew | *taufrisch sein* |
| Beauty is only skin deep. | *Schönheit ist vergänglich.* |
| a hulk of a man | *ein Kerl wie ein Baum* |
| be as flat as a pancake | *platt wie Flandern sein (keinen Busen haben)* |
| be as thin as a rake | *spindeldürr sein* |
| be a beanpole | *eine Bohnenstange / ein langer Lulatsch sein* |
| look like a drowned cat | *wie ein begossener Pudel aussehen* |
| look a sight | *einen schrecklichen Anblick bieten* |
| have a spare tyre | *einen Fettwulst / Rettungsring um den Bauch haben* |

| | |
|---|---|
| be knee-high to a grasshopper | *ein Winzling sein* |
| Hello, curly! | *Hi, Krauskopf!* |
| You look like you've been dragged through a hedge backwards. | *Du siehst aus wie durch den Wolf gedreht.* |
| Hello, half pint! | *Hallo, du halbe Portion!* |

## QUICK CHECK 9: Bob and Ron are different

**R:** You've jogged more than ten kilometres. Don't exaggerate. You're already *as thin as a* .......................... .

**B:** You should jog, too. You *cut a* .......................... *figure.*

**R:** I've been doing sports since I *was knee-high to a* .......................... .

**B:** And you're still hopping around with all your injuries.

## 4. Fine feathers make fine birds – *Kleider machen Leute*

| | |
|---|---|
| look like something that the cat dragged in | *völlig heruntergekommen aussehen* |
| dress in one's Sunday best | *im Sonntagsstaat sein* |
| be dressed to kill | *aufgedonnert / todschick gekleidet sein* |
| Fine feathers make fine birds. | *Kleider machen Leute.* |
| tog oneself out / up | *sich schick machen* |
| be spruced up | *aufgebrezelt sein* |
| get all dotted up | *sich schick anziehen* |
| look as if one has just stepped out of a fashion catalogue | *wie aus dem Ei gepellt sein* |
| be dressed to the nines | *festlich gekleidet sein; herausgeputzt sein* |
| be mutton dressed as lamb | *sich auf jung herausputzen* |
| be in one's glad rags | *die feinsten Klamotten anhaben* |
| fit someone like a glove | *jemandem wie angegossen passen* |
| It looks well on you. | *Es steht dir gut.* |
| There's no accounting for taste. | *Über Geschmack lässt sich nicht streiten.* |
| stand / stick out like a sore thumb | *auffallen wie ein bunter Hund* |
| go / be out of fashion | *aus der Mode kommen; veralten* |
| be behind the times | *altmodisch / unmodern / aus der Mode sein* |

| | |
|---|---|
| be all dressed up | *todschick gekleidet sein* |
| put on one's best bib and tucker | *den Sonntagsstaat anlegen* |
| wear hand-me-downs | *abgelegte Kleidungstücke tragen* |
| Don't judge a book by its cover. | *Man sollte nicht nach dem Äußeren gehen.* |

**QUICK CHECK 10: What's the *woggle*?**

Two female clerks discuss clothes, Sue and Jean:

**J:** My goodness, you're *all woggled up*. Have you got a job interview or what?

**S:** No, I haven't actually. I've got a dinner date.

**J:** Well, you *stick out like a sore woggle* here at work. And by the way, that sort of dress *is a bit out of woggle.*

**S:** Jean, you *are* really *behind the woggles.*

TIME FOR A SMILE

Overheard in Spaceship Enterprise approaching the Planet of the Amazons:
"Beam me down, Scotty. ... Very funny, Scotty! Now beam down my clothes as well. Quick!"

## 5. Stages of life – *Lebensabschnitte*

| | |
|---|---|
| be wet behind the ears | *noch nicht trocken hinter den Ohren sein* |
| You can't teach an old dog new tricks. | *Was Hänschen nicht lernt, lernt Hans nimmermehr.* |
| have an old head on young shoulders | *reif für sein Alter sein* |
| be in the prime of life | *in den besten Jahren sein* |
| be alive and kicking | *putzmunter / fidel sein* |
| have had a good innings | *eine schöne Zeit / ein erfülltes Leben gehabt haben* |
| I'm old enough to be your father. | *Ich könnte dein Vater sein.* |

4

| | |
|---|---|
| be over the hill | *seine besten Jahre hinter sich haben* |
| be getting on in years | *alt / älter werden* |
| be long in the tooth | *nicht mehr der Jüngste sein* |
| be no spring chicken | *kein junger Spritzer / Flitzer mehr sein* |
| take years off someone | *jemanden um Jahre jünger machen* |
| be pushing fifty | *stark auf die Fünfzig zugehen* |
| What makes someone tick. | *Das, wofür jemand lebt.* |
| Life is not all beer and skittles. | *Das Leben ist nicht das reine Honigschlecken.* |
| have had one's day | *die besten Jahre hinter sich haben* |
| She looks her age. | *Man sieht ihr das Alter an.* |
| scrape along / by | *gerade so auskommen; sich mühsam durchschlagen* |
| be past one's prime | *seine besten Jahre hinter sich haben* |
| feel one's age | *sich alt fühlen* |
| put years on | *um Jahre altern* |
| be living on borrowed time | *nicht mehr lange zu leben haben; kurz vor dem Tode stehen* |
| be as old as the hills | *steinalt / uralt sein* |
| be past it | *jenseits von Gut und Böse sein* |
| die of old age | *an Altersschwäche sterben* |
| have one foot in the grave | *mit einem Bein im Grab stehen* |
| die with one's boots on | *in den Stiefeln sterben; plötzlich mitten aus dem Leben scheiden* |

TIME FOR A SMILE

***What it means to be old***

Old is when your friends compliment you on your new alligator shoes and you are barefoot.

Old is when you remember when the Dead Sea was only sick.

Old is when your wife says "Let's go upstairs and make love" and you answer "Honey, I can't do both!"

## QUICK CHECK 11: Take a vowel for an x

Director of personnel (**D**) and personnel manager (**P**) talk about age:

**D:** So now you're sixty. I know *you're* not at all *pxst xt*, but you have to think about your pension.

**P:** You're right. I'm beginning to *fxxl my xgx.*

**D:** Well, you're *getting a bit long in the txxth.* No, that's a joke. Of course, it's the same for me. *I'm pxshxng fifty* as well.

## QUICK CHECK 12: Only one is correct

**1.** Young Tom is a chip of the old block. He and his father are both
**A.** made of the same wood.
**B.** cast in the same mould.
**C.** painted with the same brush.

**2.** Tom and his brother, however, are
**A.** as different as chalk and cheese
**B.** as different as two peas
**C.** as different as flock and feather

**3.** Ron has lost 20 kilos. He's now
**A.** as thin as a pin.
**B.** as thin as a beanpole.
**C.** as thin as a rake.

**4.** When he realized that he had lost a lot of money at the stock exchange he knew
**A.** he had egg on his face.
**B.** he wiped an egg out of his face.
**C.** looked like an egg in underware.

**5.** He tried to sell me this yellow suit. He said that
**A.** it fitted me off the peg.
**B.** it fitted me like a rag.
**C.** it fitted me like a glove.

# Talking about characters

## *Über Charaktere sprechen*

5

### BIRD'S EYE VIEW

### LEVEL I

1. *Ein guter Charakter* – A good character
2. *Ein schlechter Charakter* – A bad character

### LEVEL II

1. Talking about temperaments – *Über Temperamente sprechen*
2. People like you and me – *Menschen wie du und ich*
3. People we have to live with – *Menschen, mit denen wir leben müssen*

### TIME FOR A SMILE

The Archbishop of Canterbury was making his first visit to New York. His advisers suggested that he should be very diplomatic in answering questions from press reporters so as to avoid any controversy. There was a crowd of reporters waiting to greet him and, as he stepped from the plane, one of them thrust a microphone in his face and said, "Say, Bishop, what's your opinion on the large number of brothels in Manhattan?"
Remembering that he had to be tactful the Archbishop said cautiously, "Are there any brothels in Manhattan?"
The following morning, the headlines of the New York Times read: ARCHBISHOP'S FIRST QUESTION ON ARRIVING IN NEW YORK – "ARE THERE ANY BROTHELS IN MANHATTAN?"

## LEVEL 1

One of the authors, who was a very industrious student a few decades ago, showed a lot of courage by going to live in the Soviet Union. He liked it over there and had no problems with the ordinary people. "They are a decent lot," he would say. "But the system certainly isn't very efficient." Ron thought it would be useful for him in his later career. He was a very ambitious young fellow. Well, we all make mistakes, don't we?

### 1. *Ein guter Charakter* – A good character

| | |
|---|---|
| *aufrichtig / offen und ehrlich sein* | Is Tom completely sincere? – Yes, he's a frank and open person. |
| *charakterfest sein* | His brother, Tim has a strong character. Tom, however, has a weak character. |
| *vertrauen; vertrauenswürdig sein* | Does Tina trust Tom? – Yes, Tom is very trustworthy. |
| *fleißig sein* | Tim works more than 10 hours a day. He's very industrious. |
| *sich verlassen auf* | Tim has a strong character. I think we can rely / depend on him. |
| *offen sein; verschlossen sein* | Tim is an open character, but his wife, Tina, is very reserved. |
| *entschlossen / bestimmt sein* | Tina knows what's good for Tim. She's a very determined person. |
| *pünktlich* | Tim's new secretary Susan is very punctual. She's never late. |
| *schwer arbeiten* | Susan is a hard worker. She's very hard-working. |
| *Mut beweisen* | Tim showed great courage when he arrested the gangster. |
| *bescheiden sein* | Tim didn't want to be praised. He's a modest man. |
| *ein guter Verlierer sein* | Tom's not very good at chess. He's a fair loser. |
| *Ehrlich währt am längsten.* | Honesty is the best policy. |
| *großzügig* | He is very generous. He isn't rich, but he gives to the poor. |

| | |
|---|---|
| *für seine Großzügigkeit bekannt sein* | When I need money I ask Tom. He's known for his generosity. |
| *hilfsbereit sein* | Thank you for carrying my bags. You're really a helpful boy. |
| *jemandem treu sein* | Tom is a faithful husband. He's always been faithful to Tina. |
| *Humor haben* | Tom is a humorous fellow. He's got a good sense of humour. |
| *anständige Leute* | Our neighbours are decent people. |
| *gemäßigte Ansichten vertreten* | Bob's a man of moderate views. He's easy to get along with. |
| *gesellig sein* | Our neighbours are very sociable. They like to have guests. |
| *ein anständiger Kerl sein* | Bob's a good sport. He has his heart in the right place. |
| *jemandem die Treue halten* | Tina has always remained faithful to Tom. |
| *ein bescheidenes Leben führen* | Although he's very rich he leads a simple and modest life. |
| *sich beherrschen* | His students tried to provoke him, but Bob kept his temper. |
| *sympathisch / liebenswert sein* | I like Bob for his modesty and honesty. He's a likeable chap. |
| *ein angenehmer Mensch sein* | Tom is very popular. He has such a pleasant personality. |
| *tüchtig sein* | Tom's secretary is pretty and what is more, she's efficient. |

## QUICK CHECK 1: Tim, the yes-man

1. Do you trust Tom?
   Yes, he is very ................................................ .
2. Bob showed great courage when he arrested the gangster.
   Yes, he was very ................................................ .
3. I believe in his sincerity .
   Yes, he's completely ................................................ .
4. He's known for his generosity.
   Yes, he's very ................................................ .

### TIME FOR A SMILE

I can please only one person per day. Today is not your day. Tomorrow, isn't looking good either.

### QUICK CHECK 2: Incompatible characters

1. Bob has a *strong* character. His brother has a ......................... character.
2. Susan is very *punctual*. Her colleague is always ......................... .
3. Bob is an *open character*. His wife is very ......................... .
4. Bob works *efficiently*. Brian is a ......................... fellow.

## 2. *Ein schlechter Charakter* – A bad character

| | |
|---|---|
| *leichtsinnig mit Geld umgehen* | He's careless with money. He's a careless driver. |
| *für seine Grausamkeit bekannt sein* | Dick is cruel to animals. He's known for his cruelty. |
| *ein fauler Bursche sein* | He's a lazy fellow. He never works overtime. |
| *wütend / gereizt sein* | Dad's in a bad temper today. You'd better keep out of his way. |
| *in Wut geraten* | Tim easily loses his temper. It's hard to get along with him. |
| *seltsamer Geschmack und eigenartige Ansichten* | Dick is a strange man, with strange tastes and views. |
| *sich schlecht benehmen* | This boy has no manners. He behaves badly at table. |
| *keine Manieren haben* | Our boss is very impolite to his workers. He has no manners. |
| *ehrgeizig sein* | Tom wants to climb the ladder. He's very ambitious. |
| *sich nicht zusammenreißen können* | Dick often loses his temper. He can't pull himself together. |
| *ein übler Bursche* | Tom is a good sport (sort); his brother Dick is a bad sort. |

| | |
|---|---|
| *zu nichts taugen* | Tim's good for nothing. That's why the boss has fired him. |
| *die Frechheit haben, zu ...* | What? He had the insolence to call me a liar. |
| *oberflächlich sein* | He's not a solid author. All his essays are very superficial. |
| *gleichgültig gegenüber ... sein* | Is she a good wife? She seems indifferent to Tom's problems. |
| *eifersüchtig sein* | He's always jealous when his wife talks to other men. |
| *gierig* | Joe got richer and richer and also much greedier. |

## QUICK CHECK 3: Let's characterise them!

Match the numbers with the letters.

| | |
|---|---|
| **1.** Bill can't get enough money. | **A.** *jealous* |
| **2.** Bob made lots of silly mistakes in his essay. | **B.** *ambitious* |
| **3.** Tom doesn't care for Sue's feelings. | **C.** *superficial* |
| **4.** Ron can't sleep because of his girlfriend. | **D.** *indifferent* |
| **5.** John wants to become number 1. | **E.** *greedy* |

## QUICK CHECK 4: Get to know yourself

1. If you spend too much you're ......................... .......... money.
2. If you torture cats and dogs you're ......................... .......... animals.
3. If you never work overtime you're a .............................. fellow.
4. If you behave badly at table you have .......... ......................... .

TIME FOR A SMILE

*The Wisdom of the Scots*

Don't spend two dollars to have a shirt dry cleaned. Donate it to the Salvation Army. They'll clean it and put it on a hanger. Next morning you can buy it back for 75 cents.

## LEVEL M

Christine who works in our local tax office is *worth her weight in gold*. She is always willing to answer any silly questions I might have and she's very *quick on the uptake*. Some tax officials fob you off with forms and bureaucracy, but she seems to *have everything at her fingertips*. And I'm self-employed so there can be grey areas. So far she's always found a workable solution. There are *no flies on Christine*.

### 1. Talking about temperament – *Über Temperament sprechen*

| | |
|---|---|
| be as meek as a lamb | *sanft wie ein Lamm sein* |
| She wouldn't say boo to a goose. | *Sie könnte keiner Fliege etwas zuleide tun.* |
| Butter wouldn't melt in her mouth. | *Sie kann kein Wässerchen trüben.* |
| read someone like a book | *für jemanden wie ein offenes Buch sein* |
| wear one's heart on one's sleeve | *sein Herz auf der Zunge tragen* |
| be full of beans | *putzmunter / aufgekratzt sein* |
| be full of fight | *angriffslustig sein* |
| be a live wire | *ein Energiebündel sein* |
| have an open mind | *aufgeschlossen sein* |
| have bottle / have guts | *Mumm / Schneid haben* |
| be as cool as a cucumber | *ruhig Blut bewahren* |
| have / keep a stiff upper lip | *Haltung bewahren* |
| go native | *sich an seine Umgebung anpassen* |
| be down-to-earth | *pragmatisch / realistisch sein* |
| wear the trousers | *die Hosen anhaben; das Regiment zu Hause führen; das Sagen haben* |
| His bark is worse that his bite. | *etwa: Hunde, die bellen, beißen nicht.* |
| a rough diamond | *ein ungeschliffener Diamant* |
| a cold fish | *ein eiskalter Hund* |
| be the black sheep of the family | *das schwarze Schaf der Familie sein* |
| be as stubborn as a mule | *dickköpfig wie ein Stier / störrisch wie ein Esel sein* |

5

| | |
|---|---|
| be as hard as nails | *stahlhart sein* |
| have no drive / pep / guts | *keinen Mumm haben* |
| be as dull as ditchwater / dishwater | *sterbenslangweilig / fade / uninteressant sein* |
| a stick-in-the-mud | *eine lahme Ente* |
| live in cloud-cuckoo-land; live in a fool's paradise | *im Wolkenkuckucksheim leben* |
| have one's head in the clouds | *ein Traumtänzer sein* |
| be a wet blanket | *ein Trauerkloß / Spielverderber sein* |
| be a wimp / drip | *ein Schlappschwanz / Langweiler sein* |
| be a pain in the neck / arse (sl) | *eine Landplage / Nervensäge sein; lästig sein* |
| a smart alec; a bright spark; a clever clogs; a clever dick; a smarty pants | *ein Besserwisser / Neunmalgescheiter sein* |
| be a smart arse / ass (sl) | *ein Klugscheißer sein* |
| be as slippery as an eel | *ein aalglatter Typ sein* |
| be a nosy parker | *seine Nase überall hineinstecken* |
| be a nasty piece / bit of work | *ein übler Kunde; ein gemeiner / abstoßender Mensch sein* |
| be a snake in the grass | *eine falsche Schlange sein* |
| have a fiery temperament | *temperamentvoll sein* |

## QUICK CHECK 5: Silly questions about Betsy and Bert

1. What would Betsy not say to a goose?
2. What would not melt in her mouth?
3. Where does Bert wear his heart?
4. What is worse than his bite?

## QUICK CHECK 6: Fit these animals in

| fish | snake | eel |
|---|---|---|

Ron and Anthony discuss a former colleague:

**R:** So Duckman wants to join us again. I'm quite shocked. He deceived us once. He's *as slippery as an* .............................. .

**A:** Right, and when he first presented himself you would have thought you could *read him like an open book*. Anyway I had the feeling *he was a bit of a cold* .............................. .

**R:** And to cancel all his courses by pretending he was in hospital. *What a* .............................. *in the grass!*

## 2. People like you and me – *Menschen wie du und ich*

| | |
|---|---|
| be quick on the uptake | *schnell von Begriff sein* |
| twig (something) (sl) | *etwas kapieren* |
| have one's head screwed on the right way | *ein helles Köpfchen sein* |
| I wasn't born yesterday. | *Ich bin nicht von gestern.* |
| be as good as gold | *kreuzbrav sein* |
| to a T | *perfekt gemacht; wie angegossen; haargenau* |
| be head and shoulders above someone | *jemandem haushoch überlegen sein* |
| be worth one's weight in gold | *sein Gewicht in Gold wert sein; unbezahlbar sein* |
| be worth a fortune | *ein Vermögen wert sein* |
| be one in a million | *ein Juwel sein; unersetzlich sein* |
| keep a level head | *bei klarem Verstand bleiben* |
| keep one's wits about one | *einen kühlen Kopf bewahren* |
| be as crafty as a fox | *ein schlauer Fuchs sein* |
| have get-up-and-go / oomph | *Energie / Schwung / Pep haben* |
| think on one's feet | *schnell reagieren* |
| be up to the mark | *auf dem Laufenden sein* |
| do something with one hand tied behind one's back | *etwas mit links tun* |

| | |
|---|---|
| be able to do something standing on one's head | *etwas mit links tun können* |
| be a dab hand at something | *ein Könner sein* |
| That is my middle name. | *Das ist genau meine Stärke.* |
| know / have something off pat | *etwas parat haben; etwas auf der Pfanne haben* |
| There are no flies on him. | *Er lässt sich nicht leicht über den Tisch ziehen.* |
| (be able to) run rings around someone | *jemanden in die Tasche stecken (können); jemandem haushoch überlegen sein* |
| stand on one's own feet | *auf seinen eigenen Beinen stehen* |
| take to something like a duck to water | *sich sofort in seinem Element fühlen* |
| know the ins and outs (of something) | *sich mit einer Sache genau auskennen* |
| know what's what | *wissen, wie es in der Welt zugeht / wo's langgeht* |
| know (a place / something) like the back of one's hand | *einen Ort / Sachverhalt wie seine Westentasche kennen* |
| have something at one's fingertips | *etwas aus dem Effeff beherrschen* |
| be on the ball | *auf Draht / Zack sein* |
| know every trick in the book; know every trick of the trade | *mit allen Wassern gewaschen sein; durchtrieben sein* |
| leave no stone unturned; explore every avenue | *nichts unversucht lassen; keine Mühen scheuen* |
| move heaven and earth; pull out all the stops (do something) | *Himmel und Hölle in Bewegung setzen; sich sehr große Mühe geben* |
| do one's very / level best | *sein Bestes geben* |
| keep up with the Joneses | *den Nachbarn nicht nachstehen wollen* |

### TIME FOR A SMILE

I am desperately trying to figure out why Kamikaze pilots wore helmets. *Dave Edison*

## QUICK CHECK 7: What's the *woggle*?

Annette and Robert discuss living abroad:

**R:** You can't live abroad when you're pushing fifty. It's too late *to learn the ins and woggles* of a country, of its systems.

**A:** Well, you wouldn't, would you? One has to be quick on the *woggle* or you'll make mistakes.

**R:** Don't worry! Change and risk, *that's my middle woggle.*

## QUICK CHECK 8: Remember the animal idioms?

| | | |
|---|---|---|
| **1.** *Fliege* | *Er lässt sich nicht leicht übers Ohr hauen* | There are ........................ ........................................ |
| **2.** *Ente* | *Sie fühlte sich sofort in ihrem Element.* | She ................................ ........................................ |
| **3.** *Fuchs* | *Er ist ein schlauer Fuchs.* | He's as ........................... ........................................ |

## 3. People we have to live with – *Menschen, mit denen wir leben müssen*

| | |
|---|---|
| be bone-idle / bone-lazy | *stinkfaul sein* |
| You can't teach an old dog new tricks. | *Was Hänschen nicht lernt, lernt Hans nimmermehr.* |
| be no great shakes (at something) | *nichts Besonderes sein* |
| not make head nor tail of something / someone | *aus etwas / jemandem nicht schlau werden* |
| be nothing to write home about | *nicht das Gelbe vom Ei sein* |
| He's not all he's cracked up to be. | *Er hält nicht, was man sich von ihm verspricht. Er wird seinem Ruf nicht gerecht.* |
| not be able to hold a candle to someone | *jemandem das Wasser nicht reichen können* |
| be a loose cannon | *eine Gefahr für seine Umwelt sein* |
| be as common as muck | *Dutzendware sein; ordinär und vulgär sein* |
| There's one born every minute. | *Jeden Tag steht ein Dummer auf.* |

| | |
|---|---|
| be a bit dim | *die Weisheit nicht gerade mit Löffeln gefressen haben* |
| be blue-eyed | *blauäugig / gutgläubig sein* |
| be as thick as two short planks; be as thick as a brick (sl) | *dumm wie Bohnenstroh sein* |
| have a screw loose | *eine Schraube locker haben* |
| have bats in the belfry | *nicht alle Tassen im Schrank haben* |
| be off one's head | *einen Vogel haben* |
| be slow on the uptake | *schwer von Begriff sein* |
| be as blind as a bat | *blind wie ein Maulwurf sein* |
| have a one-track mind | *immer nur an eines denken* |
| be at one's wits' end | *verzweifelt sein; nicht mehr weiterwissen* |
| have a memory / mind like a sieve | *sehr vergesslich sein; ein Gedächtnis wie ein Sieb haben* |
| have tunnel vision | *nicht über seinen Tellerrand blicken können* |
| be (clean) round the bend / twist | *total spinnen* |
| have rocks in one's head | *verrückt / wahnsinnig sein* |
| have a shot off (sl) | *einen Dachschaden haben; nicht mehr alle Tassen im Schrank haben* |
| chase after rainbows | *Illusionen / Chimären nachjagen* |
| be all fingers and thumbs | *zwei linke Hände haben; sehr ungeschickt sein* |
| not have the foggiest idea / notion | *keinen blassen Schimmer haben* |
| not have the faintest idea / notion; not have a clue | *nicht die leiseste Ahnung haben* |
| a dead loss / turkey [US] | *ein totaler Reinfall; ein hoffnungsloser Fall; Hopfen und Malz sind verloren* |
| not do a stroke of work | *keinen Handschlag tun* |
| not be in the same league as someone | *sich mit jemandem nicht messen können* |
| not be a patch on someone / something | *an jemanden / etwas nicht heranreichen; es mit jemandem / etwas nicht aufnehmen können* |
| stick / poke one's nose into someone's business | *seine Nase in jemandes Angelegenheit stecken* |
| be a bad lot / egg | *ein übler Kunde sein* |
| be a parasite on the system | *ein Schmarotzer sein* |

## QUICK CHECK 9: Fill the gaps

The handyman. Bob and René discuss him:

**B:** So, I'm absolutely furious. My new plumber is as blind as a ................ and he's bone- ..................., too.

**R:** Bob, I warned you not to employ him. It was so clear to me that he wouldn't do a ................... of work. Poor old Bob. There's one ................... every minute.

## QUICK CHECK 10: Tim, the yes-man

Is Bert the right man?

1. **Tom:** I think Bert is too old to handle our new computer systems.
   **Tim:** Yes, you can't ......................................................... .
2. **Tom:** And he's behaving strangely. He tried to kiss my secretary.
   **Tim:** Yes, he seems to have ............................................belfry.
3. **Tom:** I'm afraid he'll be a dead loss in the computer department.
   **Tim:** Yes, he'll turn out to be ........................... , as the Americans say.
4. **Tom:** And I think he's exploiting us. He uses the company phone for private calls, does his shopping on company time etc.
   **Tim:** Yes, he's a .......................................................on the company.

### TIME FOR A SMILE

Lord Charles had employed a very young and attractive secretary. One day the girl didn't turn up for work – but her mother did. "I'm Ann's mother," she announced. "Do you realise that she's pregnant?"
"Oh, goodness," exclaimed Lord Charles, "if it's true and she's really pregnant, I'll give her fifty thousand pounds and set up a trust fund for the baby – if that's all right with you?"
"That sounds wonderful," said the mother, "and if it should turn out to be a false alarm, will you give her another chance?"

# Opinion, mind and memory

## *Meinung, Geist, Gedächtnis*

6

BIRD'S EYE VIEW

### LEVEL 1

1. *Denken und glauben* – Thinking and believing
2. *Seine Meinung ankündigen* – Offering one's opinion
3. *Unterschiedlicher Meinung sein* – Disagreeing
4. *Vorausdenken* – Thinking about the future
5. *Zurückdenken* – Thinking about the past
6. *Sich irren* – Being mistaken

### LEVEL 2

1. Using one's brains – *Sein Gehirn gebrauchen*
2. Be slow on the uptake – *Eine lange Leitung haben*
3. Remembering and forgetting – *Erinnern und vergessen*
4. Taking a stand – *Stellung beziehen*

### TIME FOR A SMILE

"My son Tom is so forgetful," complained a sales manager to his secretary, "I asked him to get me a packet of cigarettes on his way back from lunch, but I'm not even sure he'll remember to come back himself."

A few minutes later Tom dashed into the office, shouting: "Dad! At lunch I met old man Kelly, who hasn't bought a penny's worth from us in five years and before we parted I talked him into a half-a-million-dollar order!"

"What did I tell you?" sighed the sales manager, "he forgot the cigarettes!"

## LEVEL 1



Michael and Ron talk about the future of the company:

**M:** Annette is working too many hours. Think about it!

**R:** I know, but what can I do? I couldn't believe my eyes when I saw the quantity of work.

**M:** Well, as far as I am able to judge it's too much for them, but too little to employ another translator.

**R:** Actually, I don't quite agree with you. We can take work away from the free-lancers, then we'll have enough. I think we'll need to work out a plan for the future.

### 1. *Denken und glauben* – Thinking and believing

| | |
|---|---|
| *auf den Gedanken kommen / bringen* | I'm not interested in buying a house. What made you think of that? |
| *sich etwas durch den Kopf gehen lassen / überdenken* | This house in Italy is really a good bargain. Think it over. |
| *nicht im Traum daran denken* | Buying a house in Italy? I wouldn't dream of it. |
| *nicht daran denken, etwas zu tun* | I have no intention/ thought of wasting my money. |
| *Wie denkst du darüber?* | A house in Italy! How do you see it? |
| *es sich zweimal überlegen* | One should think twice about buying a house in a foreign country. |
| *sich denken können* | You should have known that I wouldn't dream of investing money in Italy. |
| *nach ernsthafter Erwägung* | However, after serious thought, Tom bought a farm in Sicily. |
| *zu dem Schluss kommen* | Two years later Tom came to the conclusion that buying a farm in Sicily hadn't been such a bad idea after all. |
| *keine Ahnung haben* | Where's Fred? – I've no idea. |
| *ob du es glaubst oder nicht* | Believe it or not, Fred has been arrested for shoplifting. |

6

| | |
|---|---|
| *Stellen Sie sich vor!* | He stole a bottle of wine. Just imagine! |
| *Das hätte ich nicht gedacht.* | I didn't think / I wouldn't have thought he was capable of shop-lifting. |
| *zu denken geben* | It makes you think, doesn't it? |
| *Wer hätte das gedacht!* | Fred – stealing a bottle of wine! Who would have thought it! |
| *an nichts anderes denken* | His one thought now is how to get out of prison. |
| *kaum zu glauben / du glaubst es nicht* | Susan, would you believe it, came to the party in a bikini. |
| *seinen Augen / Ohren nicht trauen* | I stared at her, scarcely able to believe my eyes. |
| *von Sinnen sein* | She must taken leave of her senses. Everybody arrived in evening dress and she came in a bikini. |
| *sich mit dem Gedanken tragen* | My wife had (some) thoughts of leaving the party immediately. |
| *keine Ahnung* | "Let's go," she said. – "Good idea! – But where shall we go?" – "No idea." |
| *verstehen* | I think Tom should fire Susan. – I see what you mean. |
| *nach reiflicher Überlegung* | After some thought, Tom decided to fire Susan. |
| *einen scharfen Verstand haben* | Jill has got a sharp mind and her son has a keen mind, too. |
| *gesunder Menschenverstand* | Everyone thinks that God has given him enough common sense. |
| *nachgrübeln über* | Why are you so deep in thought? – I'm brooding over my financial problems. |
| *Es ist mir nie in den Sinn gekommen, ...* | It never occurred to me that Bill might be unhappy. |

## QUICK CHECK 1: Think & Co

Do you remember those little words?

1. I'm not interested in buying a house. What made you *think* ................ that?
2. This house is really a good bargain. *Think* it .................... .
3. One should *think* twice .................... buying a house.

## QUICK CHECK 2: Translation exercise

Bob and Ron discuss the next book:

**B:** (*Nach reiflicher Überlegung*) I've decided not to meet Oro's deadlines. I haven't got time.

**R:** (*Ob du das glaubst oder nicht*), I absolutely agree with you. And I'd like to add that (*sie müssen ihren Verstand verloren haben*) setting such short deadlines.

**B:** Right! For me it's only (*gesunder Menschenverstand*) to have a bit more time and do the job properly.

### TIME FOR A SMILE

The absent-minded professor's wife went into his study and said, "Do you know it was 28 years ago today that you asked me to marry you?"
The professor looked up from his work, "And did you?"

## 2. *Seine Meinung ankündigen* – Offering one's opinion

| | |
|---|---|
| *Wenn Sie mich fragen ...* | If you ask me ... |
| *Ich würde sagen, dass ...* | I'd say that ... |
| *Ich meine, dass ...* | I feel that ...; I think that ... |
| *Ich glaube, dass ...* | I believe that ... |
| *Nun, was mich angeht, so würde ich sagen ...* | I, for my part, would say that ... |

| | |
|---|---|
| *Soweit ich dies beurteilen kann, ...* | As far as I'm able to judge ... |
| *Mir scheint, dass ...* | It seems to me that ... |
| *Ich neige zu der Ansicht, dass ...* | I tend to think that ... |
| *Wenn Sie meine Meinung wissen wollen, ich würde sagen, dass ...* | If you want to know my opinion, I'd say that ... |
| *Meiner Meinung nach ...* | In my view / opinion ... |
| *Wie ich es / die Sache sehe ...* | As I see it ... |
| *Was mich anbelangt, so glaube ich, dass ...* | As far as I'm concerned, I think that ... |
| *Ich bin ziemlich sicher, dass ...* | I'm quite sure that ... |
| *Ich bin sicher, dass ...* | I'm certain that ... |
| *Ich bin überzeugt, dass ...* | I'm convinced that ... |
| *Es ist meine Überzeugung, dass ...* | It is my conviction that ... |
| *Es ist meine feste Überzeugung, dass ...* | It's my firm belief that ... |
| *Ist Ihnen nicht klar, dass ...?* | Don't you realize that smoking is bad for your health? |
| *sich einer Gefahr bewusst sein* | Liz likes to hitch-hike, but she isn't aware of the dangers. |
| *zu schätzen wissen* | I appreciate what you've done for me. I'm very grateful. |
| *seine Meinung ändern* | When Tina has made a decision she never changes her mind. |

## QUICK CHECK 3: More of Ron's opinion

Fill in the gaps.

Well, I'm pretty .......................... that if they attack this country it means that all over the world reasonable, moderate Muslims will take sides with the extremists. *As I* .......................... *it* the West should only make targeted attacks against the terrorists. *If you* .......................... *me* some Americans *aren't at all* .......................... *of* the dangers we're facing.

## QUICK CHECK 4: Beef up your word power

Say it with a noun.

1. Tom: Do you really believe Bert is the right man for the post?
   Tim: It's my firm ......................... that he is not the right man.
2. Tom: I'm *convinced* that we'd regret it if we gave him the job.
   Tim: Yes, it is my ........................., too, that we'd regret it .
3. Tom: Well then, it's up to you to *decide* who we give the job to.
   Tim: I've already made the ......................... . I'm going to cancel this post altogether.

## 3. *Unterschiedlicher Meinung sein* – Disagreeing

| | |
|---|---|
| *Sind Sie sicher?* | Are you sure? |
| *Meinen Sie wirklich?* | Do you really think so? |
| *Ich bin nicht ganz davon überzeugt.* | I'm not totally convinced. |
| *Ich würde Ihnen gerne zustimmen. Trotzdem habe ich einige Bedenken.* | I'd like to agree. Nevertheless I have some reservations. |
| *Ich stimme mit Ihnen bis zu einem gewissen Grad überein, bin aber nicht völlig überzeugt.* | To a certain extent I agree with you, but I'm not totally convinced. |
| *Ich kann Ihnen leider nicht ganz zustimmen.* | I'm afraid I can't quite agree with you. |
| *Nehmen Sie es mir nicht übel, aber ich sehe dies etwas anders.* | With respect, I see it a little differently. |
| *Ich kann leider nicht umhin, anderer Meinung zu sein.* | I can't help feeling that I must disagree. |
| *Ehrlich gesagt, ich kann Ihre Meinung nicht teilen* | To be honest, I can't share your opinion. |

## QUICK CHECK 5: Silly questions

1. What can two people do with an opinion? They can ......................... it.
2. What can you have if you disagree? You can have some ...................... .
3. How do you see it if you don't agree? You see it a little ...................... .

## 4. *Vorausdenken* – Thinking about the future

| | |
|---|---|
| *vorausdenken* | You have to think ahead if you want to succeed. |
| *etwas im Sinn haben* | I wonder what he has in mind. He never tells me about his plans. |
| *planen; Plan* | Tom has worked out a plan for making a lot of money. |
| *es absichtlich tun* | You've ruined my car. – Sorry, I didn't do it on purpose. |
| *die Absicht haben* | We intended to go on holiday, but everything went wrong. |
| *etwas im Schilde führen* | I have to see what he has up his sleeve. You never know with him. |

## 5. *Zurückdenken* – Thinking about the past

| | |
|---|---|
| *nicht aus dem Kopf kriegen* | I can't get Sue out of my mind. |
| *zurückdenken an* | I keep thinking back to the day Sue arrived in Hollerberg. |
| *aus Erfahrung wissen* | Tom said he knew from experience that she was a prostitute. |
| *ein schlechtes Gewissen* | At first we believed him. We still have a guilty conscience about it. |
| *zur Vernunft bringen* | Tom wanted to report her to the police, but we made him see reason. |
| *ein gutes Personengedächtnis haben* | Sue's friend Jim has a good memory for faces. |
| *auswendig lernen* | And he's clever with figures. He learned the numbers of all $1000 notes by heart. |
| *aus dem Gedächtnis* | And he was able to describe the faces of the bank robbers from memory. |
| *jemandes Gedächtnis auffrischen* | He said he didn't need the photos to refresh his memory. |
| *jemandes Gedächtnis nachhelfen* | However, the photos jogged his memory. |
| *sich etwas ins Gedächtnis (zurück)rufen* | He just called their faces to mind. |
| *wenn mein Gedächtnis mich nicht trügt* | Jim married a civil servant, if memory serves me right / correctly. |

| | |
|---|---|
| *im Vollbesitz seiner geistigen Kräfte sein* | At that moment he was not of sound mind and memory. |
| *in guter (schlechter) Erinnerung haben* | I have fond / unpleasant memories of my stay at his house. |
| *berücksichtigen, daran denken* | I'd love to play tennis with you, but please bear in mind (that) this is only the second time I've played. |
| *etwas richtig wissen* | If I've got it right, his daughter lives in Mannheim. |

### QUICK CHECK 6: Is it mind or memory?

1. I can't get the bank robbery out of my ............................ .
2. The police showed me photos to jog my ............................ .
3. Normally I've got a good ............................ for faces.
4. But after a night with Sue I was not of sound ............................ and ............................ .
5. I wasn't able to describe the bank robber from ............................ .
6. I just couldn't call his face to ............................ .

## 6. *Sich irren* – Being mistaken

| | |
|---|---|
| *irrtümlich halten für* | We all mistook her for a prostitute. |
| *sich irren* | Of course, Tom was mistaken about the way Susan earned her living. |
| *sagen wollen mit* | You know, Tom has got a complex about pretty young women. – A complex, what do you mean by that? |
| *nicht einleuchten, nicht verständlich sein* | Tom and a complex? He's such a sensible guy. It doesn't make sense to me. |
| *zu töricht / albern sein* | Don't say such silly things about Tom. That's too silly for words. |
| *etwas in den falschen Hals kriegen* | John got the wrong end of the stick. |
| *sich irren* | Oh, I got it wrong, they are not so bad after all. |

### TIME FOR A SMILE

No woman has ever shot her husband while he was doing the dishes.

6

## LEVEL Ⓜ

An author thinks about his life:
Well, I'm beginning to wonder about all this work. *It's crossed my mind* that we're somehow being exploited. We're the fools at the end of the line. All the work and little reward. I can't quite make *head (n)or tail of it.* We have a time-line but each time just before the date there's a panic and everything has to be ready yesterday. Some people at the publisher's *have a memory like a sieve.* But this time I can't keep their deadline. *Not in a month of Sundays.*

### 1. Using one's brains – *Sein Gehirn gebrauchen*

| | |
|---|---|
| the triumph of mind over matter | *der Sieg des Geistes über die Materie* |
| have a good head on one's shoulders | *ein kluges Köpfchen sein* |
| have one's head screwed on (the right way) | *vernünftig und rational denken; wissen, wo's langgeht* |
| have a hot line to heaven | *das Gras wachsen hören* |
| he has a (good) head for languages | *er ist (sehr) sprachbegabt* |
| use one's loaf | *nachdenken; seinen Grips anstrengen* |
| put on one's thinking cap | *scharf über etwas nachdenken; sein Gehirn anstrengen* |
| pick someone's brains | *jemanden um Rat / Informationen bitten* |
| rack one's brains | *sich den Kopf zerbrechen* |
| It's brains you need. | *Köpfchen muss man haben.* |
| think straight | *klar denken* |
| a razor-sharp mind | *ein messerscharfer Verstand* |
| cross / enter someone's mind | *in den Sinn kommen; einem einfallen* |
| flash into / through one's mind | *eine plötzliche Eingebung haben* |
| open one's mind to | *sich zugänglich erweisen für; empfänglich sein für* |
| I see the light. | *Mir geht ein Licht auf.* |
| cotton on to something | *etwas endlich kapieren* |
| on second thoughts | *nach reiflicher Überlegung / wenn ich es mir recht überlege* |

| | |
|---|---|
| a real brain-teaser / brain-twister | *eine harte Nuss* |
| have something on one's mind | *etwas geht einem nicht aus dem Sinn* |
| have second thoughts about it | *(so seine) Zweifel darüber haben* |
| toy with the idea | *mit dem Gedanken spielen* |
| cross one's mind | *durch den Kopf gehen; auf den Gedanken kommen* |
| A penny for your thoughts. | *Ich gäbe was dafür, wenn ich wüsste, was du denkst.* |
| deep in thought | *in Gedanken (verloren)* |
| run away with an idea | *sich täuschen; fälschlicherweise glauben* |
| That's a thought. | *Das ist eine gute Idee.* |
| give thought to | *sich Gedanken machen über* |
| know what's what | *wissen, wo's langgeht* |
| clever Dick, smarty pants | *Schlauberger* |

### QUICK CHECK 7: What to do with brains / mind

1. ............................ *someone's brain*
   to question someone who knows a lot about something in order to obtain information
2. ............................ *one's brains*
   to try very hard to think of something or remember something
3. ............................ *one's mind*
   to think about something all the time and be unable to forget it even if one wants to.

## 2. Be slow on the uptake – *Eine lange Leitung haben*

| | |
|---|---|
| That's all Greek to me! | *Das sind böhmische Dörfer für mich.* |
| It's all double Dutch to me. | *Ich verstehe nur Bahnhof.* |
| I cannot make head nor tail of it. | *Ich kann daraus nicht schlau werden.* |
| I don't get it; I'm lost. | *Ich blick da nicht durch.* |
| Not quite with it today, are we? | *Du stehst wohl auf der Leitung?* |
| have a bee in one's bonnet | *einen Fimmel / Tick haben* |
| be a bit dim | *die Weisheit nicht gerade mit Löffeln gefressen haben* |

| | |
|---|---|
| be as thick as two short planks / as thick as a brick | *dumm wie Bohnenstroh / strohdumm sein* |
| be slow on the uptake | *schwer von Begriff sein* |
| He can't see the wood for the trees. | *Er sieht den Wald vor lauter Bäumen nicht.* |
| be all at sea | *verloren sein; nicht mehr weiterwissen* |
| He's not exactly an Einstein. | *Er hat das Pulver nicht erfunden.* |

## QUICK CHECK 8: Repair the idioms

1. That's all *Dutch* to me!
2. It's all double *Einstein* to me.
3. I'm not exactly a *Greek*.

### TIME FOR A SMILE

A woman answered the phone to hear a repentant voice.
"I'm sorry, darling," he said. "I have thought things over and you can have the Rolls-Royce as a wedding present, we will move to the Gold Coast, and your mother can stay with us. Now will you marry me?"
"Of course I will," she said. "And who is this speaking?"

## QUICK CHECK 9: What's the *woggle*?

Anita is talking about her estranged husband:

**R:** Penny for your *woggles*. What's in your head?
**A:** Oh, it's nothing really. I was toying with the *woggle* of getting a new flat.
**R:** Sounds great. When?
**A:** Well, it depends on my husband. He's having second *woggles* about our relationship.
**R:** Hey, Anita! Have you got a *woggle* loose? You've got to live your own life. Don't give him a second thought.

## 3. Remembering and forgetting – *Erinnern und vergessen*

| | |
|---|---|
| within living memory | *seit Menschengedenken* |
| beyond memory | *in unvordenklichen Zeiten* |
| commit something to memory | *sich etwas einprägen* |
| keep someone in mind | *an jemanden denken; jemanden bevorzugt berücksichtigen* |
| come / spring to mind | *spontan einfallen / in den Sinn kommen* |
| bear / keep something in mind | *etwas nicht vergessen* |
| ring a bell (with someone) | *bei jemandem ankommen; jemanden auf eine Idee / Einfall bringen* |
| cast one's mind back to | *in Gedanken zurückgehen zu* |
| see something in one's mind's eye | *etwas vor seinem geistigen Auge sehen* |
| if my memory serves me (right) | *wenn ich mich recht erinnere* |
| have a memory like a sieve | *ein Gedächtnis wie ein Sieb haben* |
| slip one's mind | *etwas entfällt jemandem; etwas völlig vergessen* |
| wipe something out of one's mind; wipe the slate clean | *etwas aus seinem Gedächtnis löschen; die Vergangenheit begraben* |
| take a trip down memory lane | *in Nostalgie schwelgen* |
| let bygones be bygones | *die Vergangenheit ruhen lassen* |
| Out of sight, out of mind. | *Aus den Augen, aus dem Sinn.* |
| It never entered my thoughts. | *Es ist mir nie in den Sinn gekommen.* |

### Time for a smile

At an Italian wedding ceremony the priest asked the bride, "Do you take Franco Giuseppe Antonio to be your husband?" Looking confused, she said, "Father, there's a mistake. I'm only marrying Frank."

6

## QUICK CHECK 10: What's the *woggle*?

Melissa is thinking about her arrival in Heidelberg.

It's really strange. As I walked down High Street I had the feeling I'd been here before. *It woggles to my mind* that I'd sat somewhere here in a little wine pub with a friend of mine. But *it's woggled my mind* who I was with. For some reason I can't remember. It's *as if my memory has been woggled clean*. Still, never mind. It'll come back to me later.

## 4. Taking a stand – *Stellung beziehen*

| | |
|---|---|
| nail one's colours to the mast | *Farbe bekennen* |
| come down on one or the other side of the fence | *sich für die eine oder andere Seite entscheiden* |
| take a firm / strong / tough stand on something | *sich nachdrücklich einsetzen für; Stellung beziehen* |
| That's old hat. | *Das ist ein alter Hut / kalter Kaffee.* |
| bet one's bottom dollar | *sein letztes Hemd auf etwas wetten* |
| not mince one's words | *ganz offen und unverblümt reden* |
| give someone a piece of one's mind | *jemandem gehörig die Meinung sagen* |
| not pull one's punches | *kein Blatt vor den Mund nehmen* |
| stick to one's guns | *auf seinem Standpunkt beharren; fest zu seiner Meinung stehen* |
| Not in a month of Sundays. | *Kommt gar nicht in die Tüte; niemals!* |
| You can wait till the cows come home! | *Da kannst du lange warten! / Da kannst du warten, bis du schwarz wirst!* |
| That's how I feel and I won't be changing my mind! | *So denke ich nun mal, und daran wird sich auch nichts ändern.* |
| be as sure as eggs are eggs | *so sicher sein wie das Amen in der Kirche* |

### TIME FOR A SMILE

Two business partners decided to spend one Sunday together fishing. As they sat on the bank waiting for a nibble one suddenly turned to the other.
"I think I forgot to close the office safe!" he exclaimed.
"Don't worry," said his partner, "after all, we're both here."

## QUICK CHECK 11: Translation exercise

**B:** When will the Green Party (*Farbe bekennen*) and say whether they support the USA in its war against terrorism.

**S:** Yes, it's high time they (*Stellung beziehen*) on that issue.

**B:** They are still quarrelling among themselves and we're waiting to see (*wie sie sich entscheiden*).

**S:** (*Da kannst du lange warten).* You know what they are like.

### TIME FOR A SMILE

Dear John,
I have been unable to sleep since I broke off our engagement.
Won't you forget and forgive? Your absence is breaking my heart.
I was a fool, nobody can take your place. I love you, I love you.
Marsha
PS: Congratulations on winning the Lottery.

# Those bad little feelings

## *Negative Gefühle*

7

### Bird's eye view

**LEVEL** I

1. *Enttäuschung und Abneigung* – Disappointment and dislike
2. *Sich sorgen* – Being worried
3. *Trost und Ermutigung* – Consolation and encouragement

**LEVEL** II

1. Going through a low – *Einen seelischen Tiefpunkt erreichen*
2. Fear and worry – *Angst und Sorgen*
3. Getting angry – *Wütend werden*

### Time for a smile

The new girl is standing in front of the paper shredder, looking very confused. Another secretary who's walking by says, "Do you need some help?"
The new girl says, "Yeah, how does this work?"
"It's simple." The secretary takes the important report from the new girl's hand and starts feeding it into the shredder.
The new girl says, "Thanks, but were do the new copies come out?"

## LEVEL 1

You know, you hear all sorts of nonsense on the radio. I detest it when they give us lousy information about projects and investments. But the number of complete flops is increasing all the time. Think of the money it costs us. I think we have some cause for concern. But if you start to talk about these things people tell you "Keep your hair on. There's nothing to panic about." They are all living in cloud-cuckoo land.

### TIME FOR A SMILE

***Advice to women***

Never do housework. No man ever made love to a woman because the house was spotless.

Definition of a bachelor: A man who has missed the opportunity to make some woman miserable.

The best way to get a man to do something is to suggest he is too old for it.

## 1. *Enttäuschung und Abneigung* – Disappointment and dislike

| | |
|---|---|
| *mehr erhoffen* | How was your first day at school? – I'd hoped for more. |
| *hassen* | Mum, I hate school. – Shut up, after all you're the headmaster. |
| *enttäuscht sein* | I've never been so disappointed in my life. |
| *nicht mögen* | I don't like the look of this music teacher. I dislike him intensely. |
| *nicht vertragen können* | He loves classical music, and you know I can't stand it. |
| *ablehnen, missbilligen* | He disapproves of our jazz band. |
| *verabscheuen (1)* | He's very fond of Italian music, and detests rock and jazz. |
| *verabscheuen (2)* | I loathe liars. That's why I don't want to be a politician. |

| | |
|---|---|
| *sich nichts machen aus* | I'm not keen on dancing. – I don't care for it, either. |
| *ein langes Gesicht machen* | He opened the parcel. His face fell when he saw that it was empty. |
| *Reinfall* | How was your holiday with Liz? – Well, it was a complete flop. |
| *nicht ertragen können* | I can't bear 'yes-men'. If I say no I want you to say no, too. |
| *Zeitverschwendung sein* | How was the course? – It was a total waste of time. |

## QUICK CHECK 1: Words plus prepositions

| fond | keen | care | hope | disapprove |
|---|---|---|---|---|

You know that I'm not .............. ...... going on a holiday with Tom, at all. I'd .............. for more: Italy, Spain or Portugal. I don't .............. ...... a holiday in Germany, least of all in Gelsenkirchen.
Tom, on the other hand, .............. ...... long, expensive trips. And he's very .............. ...... historic coalmines and things like that.

## 2. *Sich sorgen* – Being worried

| | |
|---|---|
| *Was bedrückt Sie?* | You don't seem to be very happy. What's bothering you? |
| *es ist beunruhigend, dass ...* | And it's a bit worrying that there are so many icebergs around. |
| *kein Grund zur Aufregung* | There's no reason to be alarmed. Everything is under control. |
| *ein kleines Problem haben* | But now we've a bit of a problem, captain. We've hit an iceberg. |
| *Grund zur Sorge haben* | We have some cause for concern. The ship is sinking. |
| *das Problem ist, dass ...* | The trouble was that our captain was drunk most of the time. |
| *besorgt sein über (1)* | And I was concerned about the fact that there were no lifeboats. |

| | |
|---|---|
| *besorgt sein über (2)* | I was also worried about the fact that the crew was drunk. |
| *nicht mehr ein und aus wissen* | The first officer was at his wits'end as well. |
| *den Kopf verlieren* | A priest shouted to the passengers: Don't lose your heads. |
| *die Hoffnung aufgeben* | He tried to calm us down. "Don't give up hope", he cried. |
| *kein Grund zur Sorge* | I can see a ship on the horizon, so there's no need to worry. |
| *zu Tode erschrocken sein* | We were frightened to death when we heard the loud explosion. |
| *sich zu Tode ängstigen* | Crew and passengers of the sinking ship were scared to death. |

## QUICK CHECK 2: Same meaning

| | |
|---|---|
| Tom's an optimist. I can't *stand* optimists. | Tom's an optimist. I can't ........................ optimists. |
| He always says there's no *reason* to *be alarmed*. | He always says there's no ................ to ........................ . |
| But there's always a reason to be *concerned* about something. | But there's always a reason to be ........................ about something. |
| Tonight I'll *frighten* Tom to death to cure him of his optimism. | Tonight I'll ......................... Tom to death to cure him from his optimism. |

### TIME FOR A SMILE

Worried young girl: "Doctor, this new diet you've put me on makes me feel so passionate and sexy that I got carried away last night and bit off my boyfriend's right ear."
Doctor: "Don't worry, it's only about forty to fifty calories."

## 3. *Trost und Ermutigung* – Consolation and encouragement

| | |
|---|---|
| *Heute läuft alles schief.* | It's one of those days. Nothing is going right today. |
| *Was ist los mit dir?* | You don't look your usual self. What's the matter with you? |
| *Reg dich nicht auf!* | I've had an accident. But keep your hair on, the car is okay. |
| *kein Grund zur Panik* | Well, we've lost our way, but there's nothing to panic about. |
| *nicht alles schwarz sehen* | Don't look on the black side of things. It'll turn out okay. |
| *Kopf hoch!* | Chin up! I assure you everything will be all right. |
| *Es gibt viel Schlimmeres.* | You will get over it. There are much worse things. |
| *Reißen Sie sich zusammen.* | There is nothing to panic about. So pull yourself together. |
| *Die Lage könnte schlimmer sein.* | We've lost a lot of money, but things could be worse. |
| *Nur Mut!* | Try to cheer up. The situation isn't as grim as you imagine. |
| *darüber hinwegkommen* | Things could be worse. Chin up, you'll get over it. |
| *Hoffen wir das Beste.* | Will he recover from his illness? – Let's hope for the best. |
| *eine Wende zum Besseren* | He's very ill, but there's hope for a turn for the better. |
| *Hoffnungsschimmer* | Don't worry. There's still a ray of hope. |
| *herzliches Beileid* | May I offer you my sincerest sympathy. |
| *Mitgefühl / Mitleid haben mit* | Tina has sympathy with Jill because she can't have a baby. |

## QUICK CHECK 3: What the priest shouted to the passengers

1. Keep your [**A.** *hair* **B.** *chin* **C.** *heads*] on.
2. Don't lose your [**A.** *chin* **B.** *hair* **C.** *heads*].
3. Don't lose hope! [**A.** *Heads up!* **B.** *Chin up!* **C.** *Hair up!*], we'll be rescued.
4. You should [**A.** *heads on* **B.** *cheer up* **C.** *chin up*]. Where there's life, there's hope.

## QUICK CHECK 4: What's the opposite?

| | |
|---|---|
| Everything is going *well* today. | Nothing is going _______ today. |
| Things could be *better.* | Things could be _______. |
| Look on the *bright* side. | Look on the _______ side. |

### TIME FOR A SMILE

A journalist asked Sir Winston Churchill why be thought he had lived so long.
"Well, I'm convinced that it's the whisky and the cigars."
"Nothing else?" the journalist wanted to know.
"Just one more thing – cancelling my voyage on the Titanic."

## LEVEL ⓘ

Bad news; Bob and Ron:

**B:** You look like someone is walking over your grave. What's up?

**R:** *I'm* absolutely *shattered.* I'm *at the end of my tether.* Our major customer has just announced a reduction of our services by 80 percent.

**B:** My God! Why?

**R:** They've got problems themselves. And now *they've got cold feet.* They're over-reacting.

**B:** Well, it's no good *getting hot under the collar.* You'll only damage your health.

### 1. Going through a low – *Einen seelischen Tiefpunkt erreichen*

| | |
|---|---|
| get out of bed on the wrong side (this morning) | *mit dem linken Fuß aus dem Bett steigen* |
| feel cheap | *sich billig / schäbig vorkommen* |
| feel bad | *sich schlecht fühlen; ein schlechtes Gewissen haben* |
| feel like a fish out of water | *sich deplatziert vorkommen; sich (äußerst) unwohl fühlen* |
| be down in the dumps / mouth | *deprimiert / traurig sein* |
| be jiggered / whacked / bushed / all in / shattered / pooped / tuckered out / fagged out | *erschöpft / erschlagen / geschlaucht / fix und fertig sein* |
| be in the doldrums | *niedergeschlagen sein; keinen Aufwind / Auftrieb haben* |
| be at one's wits' end | *mit seinem Latein am Ende sein; nicht mehr weiterwissen* |
| cry one's eyes / heart out | *sich die Augen aus dem Kopf weinen* |
| cry oneself to sleep | *sich in den Schlaf weinen* |
| be at the end of one's rope / tether | *mit seiner Kraft am Ende sein* |
| be on one's last legs | *auf dem letzten Loch pfeifen* |
| eat one's heart out | *sich vor Gram verzehren* |
| be the last nail in one's coffin | *der letzte Nagel zum Sarg sein* |

### QUICK CHECK 5: What's the *woggle*?

1. Since he left her, my secretary's been sitting at her desk *woggling* her *woggles* out.
2. She's stopped crying now, but I can see that she's *woggling* her heart out.
3. She's physically and mentally on her last *woggles* – we'll have to look for a new secretary.

### QUICK CHECK 6: Fill in the missing letters

The tax office wants extra payments for 1999. I'm really *in the d _ dr _ _ s.* I haven't got the money. I wrote to the tax office to get a postponement, but they turned me down. I *f _ _ t really c _ _ _ p.* My bank informed me that they are not in the credit business anymore. I'm really *at my w _ _ _' end.*

**TIME FOR A SMILE**

Manager to his boss: "I'm sorry that I didn't come to your birthday party. But the day before yesterday, I made a night of it, and I had one too many."
"But why apologise?" replied his boss. "You were here!"

## 2. Fear and worry – *Angst und Sorgen*

| | |
|---|---|
| get cold feet | *kalte Füße bekommen* |
| be a chicken | *ein Hasenfuß sein* |
| put the wind up someone | *jemandem Angst einjagen* |
| get the wind up | *Angst bekommen* |
| have kittens | *Zustände kriegen* |
| get goose pimples / goose bumps | *eine Gänsehaut bekommen* |
| scare / frighten the living daylights out of someone | *jemanden das Fürchten lehren / einen wahnsinnigen Schrecken einjagen* |
| frighten the life out of someone; be frightened out of one's wits | *jemandem Todesangst einjagen; vor Angst den Verstand verlieren* |
| shake like a leaf | *wie Espenlaub zittern* |
| go as white as a sheet | *weiß / blass wie ein Leichentuch werden* |

| | |
|---|---|
| There will be the devil / hell to pay. | *Da wird der Teufel los sein.* |
| scare someone stiff | *jemanden zu Tode erschrecken* |
| give someone the creeps | *jemandem eine Gänsehaut über den Rücken jagen* |
| jump out of one's skin | *erschreckt hochfahren* |
| be just the tip of the iceberg | *nur die Spitze des Eisbergs sein* |

## QUICK CHECK 7: Churchyard idioms

Some letters are out of place. Can you repair the idioms?

1. There was the *lived* to pay when we got home that night.
2. Aunt Augusta went as *thiew* as a *ethes* when we suddenly appeared in the living room. The guests left in a hurry.
3. "You're the *last lain in my fincof,*" she shouted at us and the knife gleamed in the candlelight.
4. The sight of the knife *gave me the perces.*

## QUICK CHECK 8: xs for vowels

Ignore the xs and read it.

I was walking home last night when suddenly a man jumped out of the bushes. I was *scxrxd stxff.* And he looked so aggressive. I was *shxkxng lxkx a lxxf,* but I pulled myself together. "What do you want?" I bellowed. "I've nothing mate, just had too much to drink." And he ran off. But I must say, I had *gxt gxxsx pxmplxs.*

## 3. Getting angry – *Wütend werden*

| | |
|---|---|
| grin and bear it | *gute Miene zum bösen Spiel machen; die Zähne zusammenbeißen* |
| be cheesed / browned / pissed off (sl) | *die Nase voll haben; angeödet sein* |
| cork up one's feelings | *seine Gefühle unterdrücken* |
| bottle up one's anger | *seinen Ärger hinunterschlucken* |
| grit one's teeth | *die Zähne zusammenbeißen; mit den Zähnen knirschen* |
| let / blow off steam | *Dampf ablassen; sich abreagieren* |
| get hot and bothered | *sich aufregen; wütend werden* |
| That's the last straw! | *Jetzt reicht's!* |
| lose one's cool | *die Beherrschung verlieren* |
| lose one's temper | *einen Wutanfall bekommen* |
| burn with anger | *vor Zorn beben; rot vor Wut werden* |
| be on the warpath | *auf dem Kriegspfad sein* |
| be up in arms | *in Harnisch sein; aufgebracht sein* |
| make a song and dance about something | *sich über eine Bagatellsache fürchterlich aufregen* |
| get hot under the collar | *sich extrem aufregen* |
| fly into a rage | *in Zorn geraten, einen Wutanfall bekommen* |
| flip one's lid | *einen Koller kriegen; ausflippen* |
| be in / get into a paddy | *einen Koller haben; böse werden* |
| fly off the handle | *aus der Haut fahren; in die Luft gehen; wütend werden* |
| throw a fit / tantrum | *einen Wutanfall bekommen* |
| jump out of one's skin | *aus der Haut fahren; wütend werden* |
| hit the ceiling / roof | *(vor Wut) an die Decke / in die Luft gehen* |
| blow one's stack / top | *in die Luft gehen* |
| foam at the mouth | *vor Wut schäumen* |
| pop one's cork | *einen Wutanfall kriegen* |
| seethe with rage | *vor Wut kochen* |
| do one's nut | *durchdrehen; wahnsinnig werden* |
| I could kick myself! | *Ich könnte mich ohrfeigen!; Ich könnte mich in den Hintern beißen!* |

7

## QUICK CHECK 9: Idioms from the kitchen

Here are a few hints: Deckel – Korken – Flasche (verb)

1. Instead of discussing the problem with his son, Tom ..................... up all his anger.
2. When he heard that Tom wanted to marry Susan, a prostitute, he flipped his ..................... .
3. When Tom learned that Susan already had two children he popped his ..................... .

## QUICK CHECK 10: Translation exercise

Anthony and Ron discuss Lorry, a former trainer:

**A:** So, she's going. I didn't expect it! (*Jetzt reicht's!*) It's all the fault of this law.

**R:** Well, I must say I (*habe die Beherrschung verloren*) when I heard the news. Actually I (*habe einen Wutanfall bekommen*).

### TIME FOR A SMILE

"Do you believe in life after death?" the boss asks his employee.
"Of course I do," answers the man.
"Well, I must say I'm quite relieved, because when you were at your grandmother's funeral, she phoned and asked if you could see her tomorrow."

# Feeling good about things

## *Sich rundum wohl fühlen*

8

### Bird's eye view

#### LEVEL I

1. *Etwas mögen* – Have a liking for something
2. *Sich wohl fühlen* – Feeling well
3. *Begeisterung* – Enthusiasm
4. *Lachen und scherzen* – Laughing and joking

#### LEVEL II

1. Being happy – *Glücklich sein*
2. Put some life into the party – *Stimmung machen*
3. Laughing the Anglo-Saxon way – *Lachen wie ein Angelsachse*

### Time for a smile

An American businessman was invited to the home of his English partner. The host and his wife were playing a delicate duet on their grand piano. He listened for a while and then said, "That's nice. Very nice. But back home, me and my baby, we have a piano each."

8

## LEVEL 1

Last week I met an old friend. It was a real pleasure to see him again after all these years. Kurt was a student of mine from Wuppertal. In the conversation he told me he had founded a business after finishing his studies. He'd enjoyed himself with the work, but his partner had swindled him. That's all finished now and Kurt is looking forward *to* building up his own business again.

### 1. *Etwas mögen* – Having a liking for something

| | |
|---|---|
| *Geschmack finden an* | Jim has taken a fancy to whisky. |
| *etwas (zu) schätzen (wissen)* | He appreciates it when friends offer him a bottle of malt whisky. |
| *gern mögen* | He's also fond of red wine. |
| *lieber mögen* | He prefers Italian wines to German ones. |
| *etwas lieben* | Jim has also a great love for Italian food and Italian women. |
| *eine Vorliebe haben für* | Jim has a preference for dark-haired girls. |
| *gern mögen* | He rather fancies the idea of moving to Italy one day. |
| *entzückt sein über* | His girlfriend Anna is not delighted with Jim's plans. |
| *Freude haben an etwas* | No girl gets pleasure from the fancies of her boyfriend. |

### QUICK CHECK 1: Those pesky prepositions

1. I've taken a fancy ............................... animals.
2. My wife , too, has a great love ............................... animals.
3. We're very fond ............................... our two dogs.
4. We get a lot of pleasure .................... .................... playing with them.

### TIME FOR A SMILE

Englishmen hate two things –
racial discrimination and Irishmen.

## 2. *Sich wohl fühlen* – Feeling well

| | |
|---|---|
| *sich freuen auf + -ing-Form* | I was looking forward to going to Jim's party. |
| *in blendender Laune* | All their guests arrived at the party in high spirits. |
| *es ist eine Freude / Vergnügen + ing-Form* | It is always a pleasure listening to Jim when he sings folk songs. |
| *mit sich zufrieden sein* | We applauded and Jim was very pleased with himself. |
| *froh sein* | I was glad to have been invited. |
| *sich gut unterhalten / amüsieren* | It was a wonderful party and I enjoyed myself very much. |
| *sich besser fühlen* | I'd never felt better in my life. |
| *erleichtert sein* | But I was relieved when most of the guests left at midnight. |
| *vor Erleichterung seufzen* | I heard Anna sigh with relief when we three were alone. |
| *guter Laune sein* | I'd never seen her in a better mood. |
| *strahlend vor Glück* | I wanted to find out why she was so radiant with happiness. |
| *zufrieden sein mit* | "Are you content / satisfied with your new job," I asked. |
| *im siebten Himmel* | She told me she was in the seventh heaven. She was in love with an Italian tenor. |
| *dankbar sein* | She was grateful that I wouldn't tell Jim her secret. |

## QUICK CHECK 2: Beef up your word power

Say it with the noun.

| | |
|---|---|
| Anna *was relieved* when we left. | She sighed with ................................ when we left. |
| Jim *prefers* Italian wines to German ones. | He has a ........................... for Italian wines. |
| We were *pleased* to hear Jim sing. | It is always a ............................... listening to Jim sing. |

## QUICK CHECK 3: What's the *woggle*?

1. I was *woggling* forward *to* going to Jim's party.
2. I was *woggleful* that I had been invited.
3. All the guests arrived at the party in high *woggles.*
4. It was a wonderful party and we *woggled* ourselves very much.
5. Everybody was in the seventh *woggle.*

### TIME FOR A SMILE

A group of German tourists make their way to the top of Mount Etna and look into the smoke-filled crater. One of them turns to his neighbour and says, "It looks just like hell."
The Italian guide hears this, shakes his head and mutters, "Oh, these Germans! They've been everywhere!"

## 3. *Begeisterung* – Enthusiasm

| | |
|---|---|
| *jemanden bewundern* | Joe has marrried for the third time. I admire his courage. |
| *verliebt sein in* | After years of marriage Joe is still in love with Sue. |
| *etwas sehr gern tun* | Sue and Joe love children. Sue is very keen on having a baby. |
| *ganz aus dem Häuschen sein* | He was terribly excited when Sue told him she was pregnant. |
| *vor Freude tanzen* | They sang and danced with joy. |
| *überglücklich sein* | They were overjoyed when they learned that it might be a girl. |
| *die Menge jubelt* | When Joe entered the hospital, all the doctors and nurses cheered. |
| *glücklich sein* | "You're father of twins. Don't worry, be happy!" |
| *ungeduldig sein, brennen auf* | The grandparents were eager to see the newly born babies. |
| *begeistert sein* | Joe is enthusiastic about the idea of having a large family. |

## QUICK CHECK 4: Spot the mistake

1. Old Dunbar was looking forward to be a grandfather.
2. He was keen to being the first to congratulate Joe and Sue.
3. He was eager seeing the newly born babies.
4. He gets a lot of pleasure out of his grandchildren.

## 4. *Lachen und scherzen* – Laughing and joking

| | |
|---|---|
| *Immer nur lächeln!* | Keep smiling! |
| *Lach doch mal! (Lächle!)* | Come on, give us a smile. |
| *anlächeln* | Tom smiled at me: "Are you enjoying yourself?" he asked. |
| *über das ganze Gesicht grinsen* | He was all smiles when he got out of prison. |
| *ein fröhliches Lächeln* | Tina welcomed us with a cheerful smile. |
| *über etwas kichern* | What are you sniggering at? |
| *einen Lachanfall bekommen* | She had a fit of the giggles. |
| *leise vor sich hin lachen* | She chuckled to herself when she read the letter. |
| *ihr lachte das Glück* | Fortune has smiled on her since she was born. |
| *laut lachen* | laugh out loud |
| *Wer zuletzt lacht, lacht am besten.* | He who laughs last, laughs best. |
| *Sinn für Humor* | Jesus loves you, which shows he has a good sense of humour. |

### TIME FOR A SMILE

A Texan on holiday in Italy is trying to impress his host. He brags about everything imaginable – the size of the vegetables, the size of the cattle, the size of the estates and finally, since his listener is still totally unimpressed, the size of Texas. "You know", he says, "you can get on a train and, 24 hours later, you're still in Texas."
"You know," replies the Italian, "you can do that any time in Italy!"

8

## QUICK CHECK 5: Knowing what's what

The first one has been done for you.

| chuckle | smile | grin | snigger | laugh |
|---|---|---|---|---|

| | |
|---|---|
| make the sounds and movements of the face and body that express amusement | *laugh* |
| an expression of the face showing happiness, amusement or pleasure | .......... |
| smile widely, especially with the mouth open | .......... |
| laugh quietly to oneself | |
| low unpleasant laugh, especially at something rude or at another person's troubles | .......... |

### TIME FOR A SMILE

"If you don't start working hard immediately," said the teacher, "I'm afraid that seventy percent of you won't make it this year." One of the pupils exclaimed, "What? Seventy percent? But there aren't that many of us."

**LEVEL** (m)

8

We all go through difficult phases in life. You're fifteen years old. *The world is your oyster.* Then you study and you've got a degree. *You're on cloud nine.* Mid-twenties you *fall head over heels in love,* or at least you think you do. Three years later it's finished. Then it's your career. And for no reason at all something else goes wrong. Then *there's nothing to laugh about.*

## 1. Being happy – *Glücklich sein*

| | |
|---|---|
| That's a weight from my shoulders. | *Ein Stein fällt mir vom Herzen.* |
| see everything through rose-coloured glasses | *alles durch eine rosa Brille sehen* |
| be in fine fettle | *sich in guter Verfassung befinden* |
| be in a good mood | *gut gelaunt / aufgekratzt sein* |
| be riding high | *in Hochstimmung sein* |
| brim over with life / joy / happiness | *vor Lebensfreude / Glück überschäumen* |
| The world is your oyster. | *Die ganze Welt steht Ihnen offen.* |
| The sky's the limit. | *Die Möglichkeiten sind unbegrenzt. Die Welt liegt (einem) zu Füßen* |
| weep tears of joy | *Freudentränen weinen* |
| be tickled pink; be really chuffed | *sich wahnsinnig über etwas freuen* |
| be thrilled to bits | *überglücklich sein* |
| A dream has come true. | *Ein Traum ist wahr geworden.* |
| be as happy as a lark; as happy as a sandboy | *sich wie ein Schneekönig freuen* |
| be as pleased as punch | *überglücklich sein* |
| go overboard for / about some-one / something | *wegen etwas ausflippen; sich für etwas / jemanden überschwänglich begeistern* |
| be over the moon with / at / about something | *außer sich vor Freude sein; vor Freude ganz aus dem Häuschen sein* |
| be on cloud nine | *im siebten Himmel / auf Wolke sieben sein* |

| | |
|---|---|
| walk on air | *im siebten Himmel sein* |
| go wild over | *wahnsinnig begeistert sein* |
| fall / be head over heels in love | *bis über beide Ohren verliebt sein* |
| have a crush on someone | *in jemanden verknallt sein* |
| Life's not a bed of roses. | *Das Leben ist kein Honigschlecken.* |
| warm the cockles of someone's heart | *jemanden mit Freude und Genugtuung erfüllen* |

## QUICK CHECK 6: Beware of false friends

**1.** Tina doesn't know I'm in love with her.
**A.** over the ears
**B.** head over ears
**C.** head over heels

**2.** She told me she doesn't hate me. That's a weight from my
**A.** shoulders.
**B.** heart
**C.** neck.

**3.** I'm happy as a
**A.** snowking
**B.** snowboy
**C.** sandboy.

**4.** I'll tell her that I love her and we'll both be on
**A.** cloud nine
**B.** cloud seven
**C.** shroud nine.

## QUICK CHECK 7: Remember the idioms?

At the party. Jenny and Paula:

**P:** Wow Jenny, I think Ron (*ist in dich verknallt*). He's really staring at you.
**J:** Oh, that's not true. He's (*im siebten Himmel*) at the moment because he's just passed his university degree.
**P:** Oh, has he? With a degree, (*liegt [ihm] die Welt zu Füßen*) for him, that's true enough.
**J:** Paula, are you jealous?

## 2. Putting some life into the party – *Stimmung machen*

| | |
|---|---|
| He's good fun. | *Er ist ein lustiger Typ.* |
| be the life and soul of the party | *eine Stimmungskanone sein* |
| play / act the fool | *den Hanswurst spielen* |
| pull someone's legs | *jemanden veräppeln; jemanden aufziehen* |
| poke fun at someone | *sich über jemanden lustig machen* |
| have someone on | *jemanden auf den Arm nehmen* |
| take the mickey out of someone | *jemanden aufziehen / veräppeln* |
| crack a joke | *einen Witz reißen / verzapfen* |
| be as merry as a lark / cricket | *kreuzfidel sein* |
| have a field day | *großen Spaß haben* |
| have a ball / whale of a time | *sich riesig amüsieren* |
| jump / leap for joy | *vor Freude hüpfen* |
| shout for joy | *einen Freudenschrei ausstoßen* |
| have the time of one's life | *sich köstlich amüsieren* |
| let one's hair down | *alle Hemmungen über Bord werfen; aus sich herausgehen* |
| whoop it up | *einen draufmachen* |
| let it all hang out | *auf den Putz hauen* |
| paint the town red | *eine Sauftour machen* |
| He's not to be trifled with. | *Mit ihm ist nicht zu scherzen.* |
| take a joke | *einen Spaß / Scherz verstehen* |
| get a kick out of doing something | *an etwas mächtig Spaß haben* |
| keep a straight face | *keine Miene verziehen* |
| Seriously now! Joking aside! | *Spaß beiseite!* |

## QUICK CHECK 8: Parts of the body

**1.** Bill was the life and ............................... .
**2.** After the first drink he let his ...............................down.
**3.** And he pulled all the girls' ............................... .

## QUICK CHECK 9: What's the *woggle*?

At the party, Bob and Nick discuss Phil:

**B:** I didn't like him when I first met him, but he's certainly *the woggle and soul of the party.*

**N:** You can say that again. And everybody seems to be *having a woggle.*

**B:** But I don't feel very relaxed myself.

**N:** I noticed that. You don't seem able to *woggle a kick out of* anything. Try this pill.

## 3. Laughing the Anglo-Saxon way – *Lachen wie ein Angelsachse*

| | |
|---|---|
| laugh up one's sleeve | *sich ins Fäustchen lachen* |
| laugh behind one's hand | *heimlich / hinter vorgehaltener Hand lachen* |
| be all smiles; be beaming all over one's face | *über das ganze Gesicht strahlen* |
| double up with laughter | *sich einen Ast lachen* |
| crease up with laughter | *sich schieflachen* |
| split one's sides with laughter | *sich vor Lachen den Bauch halten* |
| burst one's sides with laughter | *sich nicht mehr halten können vor Lachen* |
| laugh one's head off | *sich totlachen* |
| die of laughter | *sich totlachen; sich kranklachen* |
| nearly die laughing; kill oneself laughing | *sich kaputtlachen* |
| be / have someone in stitches | *sich vor Lachen kugeln* |
| bray with laughter | *vor Lachen wiehern* |
| grin like a Cheshire cat | *grinsen wie ein Honigkuchenpferd* |
| laugh till the tears come | *Tränen lachen* |
| laugh at the other side of one's face | *jemandem vergeht das Lachen* |
| have a laugh at someone's expense | *schadenfroh über jemanden lachen* |
| There's nothing to laugh about. | *Da gibt es nichts zu lachen.* |

## QUICK CHECK 10: Complete the idioms

1. ............................... sleeve
2. ............................... cat
3. ............................... expense

## QUICK CHECK 11: Silly questions

1. What did he laugh off?
2. What did he burst with laughter?
3. Which side of his face did he laugh at?

## QUICK CHECK 12: What's the *woggle*?

Bob and Nick on humour:

B: You've got no sense of humour. When someone tells a funny joke you *keep a woggle face.* When there's nothing to laugh about you *split your woggles laughing.*

N: It's no good *woggling with laughter* when other people are suffering. I'm just not willing to do that.

# Being surprised and shocked

## *Überrascht und schockiert sein*

9

### BIRD'S EYE VIEW

**LEVEL**

1. Leicht überrascht sein – *Being mildly surprised*
2. Verblüfft und schockiert sein – *Being amazed and shocked*

**LEVEL**

1. Surprise! Surprise! – *Was für eine Überraschung!*
2. Be taken by surprise – *Von Ereignissen überrascht werden*
3. Exclamations of surprise – *Ausrufe des Erstaunens*

**TIME FOR A SMILE**

"I've just had a terrible shock. I have discovered that my wife is a liar."
"How do you know?" asked his mate.
"She said she was out with Betty last night."
"How do you know she wasn't?"
"Because I was out with Betty last night!"

## LEVEL 1



Actually, I was in my cottage when suddenly there was a loud bang. I was flabbergasted. It sounded as if it were inside the cottage. I went into the bedroom. There was a movement in the corner. I stood aghast. Something suddenly ran up the wall. Something shot through the room. And it had a long tail. To my dismay it jumped onto my shoulder. And it clung there for half a minute. I couldn't believe my eyes. It was a grey squirrel.

### 1. *Leicht überrascht sein* – Being mildly surprised

| | |
|---|---|
| *Was für eine Überraschung!* | A man tapped me on the shoulder: "Is that you, Al? What a surprise!" |
| *seinen Augen nicht trauen* | It was Joe! I couldn't not believe my eyes. |
| *erstaunt sein* | I was astonished when I saw that the woman at his side was Tina, my ex-wife. |
| *Das hatte ich nicht erwartet.* | I hadn't expected to see Tina in Berlin. I hadn't seen her for ages. |
| *überraschenderweise* | Surprisingly she didn't seem to recognize me. |
| *Damit hätte ich ja nicht gerechnet.* | I just said, "Well, that's a little bit of a surprise, Tina, isn't it?" |
| *zu meiner Verwunderung* | To my astonishment Tina didn't seem to recognise me. |
| *überrascht sein* | "Don't be surprised, sir!" she said, "I'm only a robot." |
| *Mich wundert gar nichts mehr.* | A robot that can speak? Well, nothing will surprise me anymore. |
| *es ist verblüffend* | "It's really amazing, isn't it?" said Joe, "Doesn't it look like Tina?" |
| *sehr erstaunt / verblüfft sein* | "You'd be amazed to see what she's able to do," he added. |
| *zu meiner Verwunderung* | "To my amazement Tina, I mean the robot, began to ... Well, that was the moment when I lost my memory, Doctor." |

## QUICK CHECK 1: Beef up your word power.

Find the noun.

| | |
|---|---|
| I was *astonished* when I saw Tina with another man. | To my ............................ Liz took off all her clothes. |
| I was *surprised* to meet Joe in Berlin. | What a ............................! I haven't seen you for ages. |
| You'd be *amazed* to see what the robot is able to do. | To my ............................ the robot began to speak. |

## 2. *Verblüfft und schockiert sein* – Being amazed and shocked

| | |
|---|---|
| *Du wirst dich wundern.* | I have to tell you something. You won't believe it. It was a shock! |
| *ein Schlag aus heiterem Himmel* | I met Joe in Berlin. That was a shot / bolt from out of the blue. |
| *Wirklich? Was Sie nicht sagen!* | Joe? Oh really? You don't say. He can't have survived. |
| *seinen Augen nicht trauen* | I stared at him, scarcely able to believe my eyes. |
| *an ein Wunder grenzen* | He looked twenty years younger. It's a near-miracle. |
| *platt sein* | I stared at him, flabbergasted. We all thought he was dead. |
| *Mein Gott, stimmt das?* | Jesus, is that really true? |
| *sprachlos / verblüfft sein* | Yes, ask Tina. We were both completely dumbfounded by his appearance. |
| *jemand anderem etwas weismachen* | Go and tell it to the marines! Nobody can survive such an explosion. |
| *wie ein Schock sein* | Joe did! It came as shock to me and Tina. |
| *ganz entgeistert sein* | Tina stood aghast as if she had seen a ghost. |
| *sprachlos sein* | She was speechless for the rest of the evening. |
| *etwas nicht fassen können* | Joe alive? I can't get over it. |

| | |
|---|---|
| *verwirrend* | He has changed his names and addresses with bewildering rapidity. |
| *sehr überrascht sein* | Joe was astounded to see us in Berlin. |
| *ziemlich schockiert sein* | He seemed taken aback that I recognized him. |
| *verwirrt sein* | I was totally bewildered because Joe's voice had changed, too. |
| *bestürzt / entsetzt sein* | The boss, too, was dismayed when I told him the story. |
| *zu seinem Entsetzen* | To his utter dismay, he received a fax signed by Joe. He wants to kill us all. |

## QUICK CHECK 2: Find the mistakes

1. He *stood aghost* at the sight of Joe's ghost.
2. That *was a shock* from the blue.
3. It *came as a shot* for all of us.
4. He, too, seemed *taken back* that we had recognized her.

## QUICK CHECK 3: Decisions! Decisions!

1. Suddenly I saw Joe. That was a shot from the
   **A.** cloud / **B.** sky / **C.** blue.
2. He had survived. It's a
   **A.** next- / **B.** close- / **C.** near-miracle.
3. That can't be true. Go and
   **A.** tell it to the marines / **B.** talk to the marines / **C.** say it to the marines.
4. I can't get
   **A.** round it / **B.** over it / **C.** on top of it

## Time for a smile

When the boss came into the office fifteen minutes early one morning, he surprised the office manager locked in fond embrace with his personal assistant. "Dobson!" thundered the boss, "You're not paid to do this, you know!"
"I know, sir," replied Dobson. "But I don't mind."

## 9 LEVEL ⓜ

Sally had lived in Battle in the countryside for years. But what a *turn-up for the books.* From one day to the next she moved to London. You could've *knocked us all down with a feather.* She's such a country girl. "Why do you want to live in the smoke, in London?" I asked her. "Oh, it all came *like a bolt from the blue.* I saw my life passing away. No culture, no adventure, only cows and sheep. So I wanted a change."

### 1. Surprise! Surprise! – *Was für eine Überraschung!*

| | |
|---|---|
| let the cat out of the bag | *die Katze aus dem Sack lassen* |
| have a surprise in store for someone | *eine Überraschung für jemanden auf Lager haben* |
| be a turn-up for the books | *eine Riesenüberraschung sein; eine unerwartete Wendung nehmen* |
| be gob-smacked (sl) | *von den Socken sein* |
| drop a bombshell | *eine Bombe platzen lassen* |
| be staggered | *Bauklötze staunen* |
| his eyes popped out of his head | *die Augen fielen ihm aus dem Kopf* |
| be for the high jump | *sich auf etwas (eine Standpauke) gefasst machen* |
| pull a long face | *ein langes Gesicht ziehen / machen* |
| laugh on the other side of one's face | *das Lachen vergeht einem* |
| be floored | *baff sein* |
| You could have knocked me down with a feather. | *Sachen gibt's, die gibt's gar nicht; das hätte mich beinahe umgehauen.* |
| Of all things! | *Ausgerechnet das!* |
| Fuck my boots! (sl) | *Menschenskind! Donnerlüttchen!* |
| The scales fall from my eyes | *Es fiel mir wie Schuppen von den Augen.* |
| I just don't believe it! You're having me on! | *Wollen Sie mir etwas weismachen?* |
| catch someone red-handed | *jemanden in flagranti erwischen* |

## QUICK CHECK 4: What's the woggle?

Naughty teacher. Tess and Ron are talking:

**R:** A friend of mine phoned me today. He *dropped a real woggle* about Phil, our former teacher.

**T:** Really? What did he say?

**R:** He said that Phil was in prison. I don't know what for.

**T:** Well, *that's a turn-up for the woggle.* Or rather it isn't really. I could have expected it. I can tell you some more things.

## 2. Being taken by surprise – *Von Ereignissen überrascht werden*

| | |
|---|---|
| take someone unawares | *jemanden unvorbereitet (an)treffen* |
| be caught by the rain | *vom Regen überrascht werden* |
| be taken by surprise | *für jemanden völlig überraschend kommen* |
| catch someone napping | *jemanden bei etwas erwischen / überraschen* |
| be overtaken by events | *von den Ereignissen überrollt werden* |
| be / come like a bolt from out of the blue | *aus heiterem Himmel kommen* |
| come out of nowhere | *aus heiterem Himmel kommen* |
| speak / talk of the devil (and he will appear) | *Wenn man vom Teufel spricht, ...* |
| Fine mess that! | *Das ist ja eine schöne Bescherung!* |
| God, that was all too much for me. | *Das war alles zu viel für mich.* |
| It all went too fast for me. | *Für mich ging das alles zu schnell.* |
| I was completely floored by the news of his death | *Sein Tod hat mich umgehauen.* |

## QUICK CHECK 5: Take a vowel for an x

Ron discusses house prices with Ann:

**R:** They've reduced interest rates by one percent. It *txxk me completely xnxwxrxs.*

**A:** Yes. I know. That decision *came xxt of the blxx,* but it's great for us anyway.

**R:** That's right. We'll be able to save. And not before time. I was *completely flxxrd* when I lost my job.

**A:** Well, you've no need to worry now. We'll soon be on top again.

## 3. Exclamations of surprise – *Ausrufe des Erstaunens*

| | |
|---|---|
| Great Scott! | *Großer Gott! Mensch Meier!* |
| Stone the crows! / Cor! / Cor blimey! | *Ach du grüne Neune!* |
| Holy smoke! / Holy cow! / Holy mackerel! | *Ach du heiliger Strohsack!* |
| Well, I never did! | *Das hätte ich ja nie für möglich gehalten!* |
| I didn't expect to hear that. | *Das hätte ich jetzt nicht gedacht.* |
| Why / how / who / when on earth / the dickens? | *Warum / wie / wer / wann in aller Welt / zum Teufel?* |
| Really? | *Im Ernst? / Wirklich?* |
| Remarkable! | *Beachtlich!* |
| Well, fancy that! | *Stell dir vor! Na so was!* |
| Good heavens! | *Meine Güte!* |
| Are you kidding? | *Machst du Witze?* |
| Are you serious? | *Im Ernst?* |
| Marvellous! | *Wunderbar! Großartig!* |
| Incredible! | *Unglaublich!* |
| That beats everything! | *Das ist einmalig / unerhört!* |
| Would you believe it! | *Was Sie nicht sagen! / Kaum zu glauben!* |
| You don't say! | *Was Sie nicht sagen!* |
| I'll be damned! | *Das gibt's doch nicht!* |
| I'll be blowed! Well, blow me! | *Menschenskind! / Donnerwetter!* |
| What the devil / hell ...? | *Was zum Teufel ...?* |
| I'll be fucked / buggered! (sl) | *Das ist ja unglaublich!* |

## QUICK CHECK 6: Odd man

One exclamation is wrong. Which?

**1.**
**A.** Are you kidding?
**B.** Are you serious?
**C.** Are you damned?

**2.**
**A.** Good heavens!
**B.** Good sky!
**C.** Great Scott!

**3.**
**A.** Holy smoke!
**B.** Holy cow!
**C.** Holy crows

## QUICK CHECK 7: Beef up your word power

Find a phrase that has almost the same meaning.
Jack meets Alex in the middle of the jungle:

**J:** *Well, blow me /* ........................ What are you doing here?
**A:** *What the devil /* ........................ are you doing here? I might ask the same question.
**J:** I'm searching for rare fruit juices that will stimulate my mind.
**A:** *Are you joking /* ........................? In the depths of the jungle?

### TIME FOR A SMILE

***A stewardess remembers***

A fellow tried to get on a British Airways flight with a little Yorkshire terrier in his arms. The stewardess told him that dogs were not allowed on board, so he went to the airport shop and bought himself a pair of dark glasses and a white walking-stick. This time he was greeted by another stewardess who said, "It's quite unusual to see a Yorkshire terrier as a guide-dog, sir. They're usually Golden Labradors."
"You mean this isn't a Golden Labrador?" said the man in surprise.

# Good luck, bad luck and how we see it

*Glück und Unglück, so wie wir es sehen*

10

## Bird's eye view

### LEVEL I

1. *Ein geborener Verlierer* – A born loser
2. *Bob, der Glückspilz* – Bob, the lucky devil

### LEVEL II

1. Idioms for optimists – *Redewendungen für Optimisten*
2. Idioms for pessimists – *Redewendungen für Pessimisten*
3. Words of comfort – *Tröstliche Worte*

### Time for a smile

***Bad luck***

Many years ago I chased a woman for almost two years, only to discover that her tastes were exactly like mine: we both were crazy about girls. *Groucho Marx*

**LEVEL** 10

I used to think that if you work hard you will succeed with things. But I guess that's just a bit naïve. Bob's always telling me that I'm a born pessimist. But he doesn't understand that you have to be prepared for the worst. And in my case it came. I must say I find it very difficult to look on the bright side. Perhaps I should try my luck with something else, like bank robbery.

## 1. *Ein geborener Verlierer* – A born loser

| | |
|---|---|
| *der geborene Pessimist* | Ron is the born pessimist. |
| *alles schwarz sehen* | He sees everything black. |
| *mit dem Schlimmsten rechnen* | He always expects the worst. |
| *auf das Schlimmste gefasst sein* | And he's prepared for the worst. |
| *die Tage sind gezählt* | He has good business going. But he insists that his company's days are numbered. |
| *etwas instinktiv fühlen; etwas vorausahnen* | "Our days are numbered. I can feel it in my bones," he tells everybody. |
| *zu einem/einer Wahrsager(in) gehen* | It's because he went to a fortuneteller. |
| *die Zukunft lesen* | It was a lady who said she could read the future. |
| *jemandem wahrsagen; die Zukunft vorhersagen* | He asked her to tell him his fortune. |
| *Es steht in den Sternen.* | "It's all in the stars," she told him. |
| *unter einem unglücklichen Stern geboren sein* | "And you were born under an unlucky star." |
| *eine Chance leichtfertig vergeben* | "You threw away a chance when you refused to marry Cathy, the baker's daughter." |
| *ein harter Schlag* | "It was a blow for the poor thing, I'm sure you remember." |
| *jemandem durch die Lappen gehen* | "You let the chance of a lifetime slip right through your fingers." |

| | |
|---|---|
| *auf die falsche Karte / das falsche Pferd setzen* | "Instead you bet on the wrong horse by marrying a banker's daughter." |
| *jemanden ins Unglück stürzen* | "You'll bring disaster (up)on your company and family," she went on. |
| *auf keinen grünen Zweig kommen* | And indeed, Ron did not get anywhere. |
| *der geborene Verlierer sein* | That is why Ron thinks he is the born loser. |

## QUICK CHECK 1: What's the opposite?

| | |
|---|---|
| be the born *winner* | be the born ...................... |
| expect the *best* | expect the ...................... |
| born under *a lucky* star | born under an ................. star. |
| bet on the *right* horse | bet on the ....................horse |

### TIME FOR A SMILE

Optimist: someone who goes into a restaurant and orders oysters, hoping to find a pearl with which to pay for the meal.

Pessimist: someone who looks around for a coffin when he smells flowers.

## 2. *Bob, der Glückspilz* – Bob, the lucky devil

| | |
|---|---|
| *ein Sonntagskind sein* | Bob was born on a Sunday, born under a lucky star. |
| *blindes Vertrauen haben in* | And he had a blind faith in his lucky star. |
| *positiv denken* | "Think positive!" was Bob's motto. |
| *mit einem silbernen Löffel im Mund geboren werden* | That's easy when you're born with a silver spoon in your mouth. |
| *alles durch eine rosarote Brille sehen* | He saw everything through rose-coloured glasses. |
| *den Dingen das Beste abgewinnen* | He always looked on the bright side of life. |
| *das Schicksal herausfordern* | He had a bad car accident, but he tempted fate and took part in a 48-hour rally. |

| | |
|---|---|
| *Der Blitz schlägt nicht zweimal an der gleichen Stelle ein.* | "Lightning never strikes twice," he told his mother when he bought the rally car. |
| *die Daumen drücken* | "Keep your fingers crossed for me, mother," he said. |
| *das große Los ziehen* | One day Tom hit the jackpot. He married Cathy the baker's daughter. |
| *Glückstreffer* | It was a stroke of luck. |
| *Einem geschenkten Gaul schaut man nicht ins Maul.* | "She isn't pretty, but you don't look a gift horse in the mouth," he used to say. |
| *sein Glück versuchen bei* | My friend Bob tried his luck with a banker's daughter. |
| *das Glück lächelt einem* | His motto: "I don't take risks as long as fortune smiles at me." |

## QUICK CHECK 2: Colourful phrases

1. Always look on the ........................ side of life.
2. He sees everything ........................ .
3. He saw everything through ........................-coloured glasses.

## QUICK CHECK 3: Violent phrases

1. Bankruptcy came as a heavy ........................ for Ron.
2. But lightning never ........................ twice.
3. In November 2001 Ron ........................ the jackpot.
4. It was a ........................ of luck.

### TIME FOR A SMILE

Optimist: a fellow who believes what's going on will be postponed.
*Kin Hubbard*

Pessimist: a man who thinks all women are bad.
An optimist hopes so.

10

## LEVEL ⓘ

To continue my story, well our little company is in bad condition. Nevertheless we have to *keep our peckers up* and try to find more customers. Perhaps we can get in somewhere by *some sort of fluke.* Bankruptcy is staring us in the face and it'll be *a close shave* whether we survive or not. I hope the whole lot won't *go down the swanny.*

### 1. Idioms for optimists – *Redewendungen für Optimisten*

| | |
|---|---|
| have a shot at something | *sein Glück versuchen* |
| Touch wood! / Knock on wood! | *Toi, toi, toi! / Dreimal auf Holz klopfen!* |
| do something on the off-chance | *etwas auf gut Glück / aufs Geratewohl tun* |
| take a chance on it | *es auf gut Glück versuchen* |
| Let's take pot luck. | *Lassen wir uns überraschen. / Versuchen wir's auf gut Glück.* |
| Good luck! / Best of luck! | *Viel Glück!* |
| be in luck | *Glück haben* |
| by a fluke | *durch einen glücklichen Zufall* |
| strike it lucky | *Glück / Dusel haben* |
| be jammy | *Schwein / Glück haben* |
| be a jammy / lucky bastard | *mehr Glück als Verstand haben* |
| That takes the cake. | *Das ist der Gipfel / die Höhe.* |
| live in clover | *in der Wolle sitzen; üppig leben* |
| come in handy | *gelegen kommen* |
| count one's blessings | *von Glück reden können; mit dem Vorhandenen zufrieden sein* |
| as luck would have it | *wie es der Zufall so wollte* |
| get to the top of the tree | *den Gipfel des Erfolgs erreichen* |
| Fortune favours fools. | *Mancher hat mehr Glück als Verstand! Gott ist mit den Dummen!* |
| That was the eleventh hour! | *Das war fünf Minuten vor zwölf / kurz vor knapp!* |
| have a close shave / call | *mit knapper Not davonkommen* |
| always land on one's feet | *immer (wieder) auf den Füßen landen* |
| have a guardian angel | *einen Schutzengel haben* |
| Keep your pecker up! | *Halt die Ohren steif!* |

## QUICK CHECK 4: Your choice

1. Das war fünf Minuten vor zwölf.
   **A.** That was five minutes to twelve!
   **B.** That was the eleventh hour!
   **C.** That was the twelfth hour!

2. Das war knapp. Ron ist noch mal davongekommen.
   **A.** That was a close shave.
   **B.** He did it on the off-chance.
   **C.** That was close haircut.

3. Ron is a lucky devil after all. Er hat den Vogel wieder mal abgeschossen.
   **A.** He took the cake again.
   **B.** He hit the bird again.
   **C.** He took pot luck again.

## QUICK CHECK 5: Silly questions

1. Where should you always land?
2. What should you knock on!
3. What should you always keep up?
4. What does fortune favour?

### Time for a smile

"What are you buying your wife for her birthday?" an Irishman from Cork asked his friend.
"Some toilet water," said the second Irishman, "but I'm told it's very expensive – up to £5 a bottle."
"Why don't you come home to my house," said the first Irishman, "and you can have all you want for free."

10

## 2. *Idioms for pessimists* – Redewendungen für Pessimisten

| | |
|---|---|
| not have a snowball's chance in hell | *nicht den Hauch einer Chance haben* |
| It never rains but it pours. | *Ein Unglück kommt selten allein.* |
| The cards are stacked against me. | *Die Karten sind gegen mich.* |
| Hard lines! / cheese! | *Das ist Pech! / Ein schwerer Schlag!* |
| be living on borrowed time | *jeden Augenblick sterben / untergehen können* |
| It was in / on the cards. | *Das musste ja passieren! Das war ja vorauszusehen!* |
| be down and out | *erledigt / kaputt / fertig sein* |
| go by the board | *zu Grunde gehen; scheitern* |
| have sweet Fanny Adams | *kein Geld / gar nichts haben* |
| push one's luck | *das Schicksal (zu sehr) herausfordern* |
| come to a sticky end | *ein böses Ende nehmen* |
| the straw that broke the camel's back | *der Tropfen, der das Fass zum Überlaufen brachte* |
| have / be a bad break | *einen Rückschlag erleben* |
| get more than one bargained for | *mehr Probleme kriegen, als man erwartet hatte* |
| be down on one's luck | *eine Pechsträhne haben* |
| jump out of the frying pan into the fire | *vom Regen in die Traufe kommen* |
| go down the river / swanny / drain | *vor die Hunde / den Bach runtergehen* |
| bite off more than one can chew | *sich übernehmen; sich zu viel zumuten* |
| be up to one's neck in trouble / shit (sl) | *bis zum Hals in Schwierigkeiten / in der Scheiße stecken* |
| have a run of bad luck | *ein Pechsträhne haben* |
| be down on one's luck; be out of luck | *kein Glück mehr haben* |
| His luck has run out. | *Seine Glückssträhne ist zu Ende.* |
| have a good (bad) hand | *gute (schlechte) Karten haben* |
| be dealt a lousy hand | *schlechte Karten bekommen* |
| draw lots | *losen; Strohhalme / Streichhölzer ziehen* |
| hope for the best | *das Beste hoffen* |
| Bankruptcy is staring us in the face. | *Die Pleite steht uns ins Haus.* |

## QUICK CHECK 6: Something went wrong here

Can you put it right?

Alan and Ron discuss their business:

**A:** I think you *bit off more than you can digest* with those courses.

**R:** Well, I had to try. I hadn't expected so much bad luck. *It never rains but it snows.*

**A:** I had *a strand of bad luck* last year too, but you just have to keep your head down and *wait for the best.*

## QUICK CHECK 7: Tim, the 'yes-man'

**Tom:** This was a black Friday at the Stock Exchange, Tim. Hard lines!

**Tim:** Yes, the cards were stacked against us. Hard ......................., indeed!

**Tom:** I'm afraid the new office will have to go by the board. We simply can't afford it.

**Tim:** Yes, we haven't got a penny. We've got sweet ............. .............. .

**Tom:** I don't think we'll be able to survive. No chance!

**Tim:** Right! We haven't got a ................... chance in .......................... .

### TIME FOR A SMILE

***Good luck – bad luck***

The glazier's bad luck: After having replaced 44 panes, he noticed that his glasses had a crack.

Fred is lucky. He has got a wife and a transistor, and they both work.

Bad luck: If you lose your wallet, it will have more money in it than it has had in the past five years.

## 3. Words of comfort – *Tröstliche Worte*

| | |
|---|---|
| Every cloud has a silver lining. | *Nach Regen kommt auch wieder Sonnenschein.* |
| Put a good / brave face on the matter! | *Mach gute Miene zum bösen Spiel!* |
| You're none the worse for it. | *Du bist nicht übler / schlechter dran.* |
| Put a bold face on it! | *Nimm's gelassen! Lass dir nichts anmerken!* |
| It'll be all right on the night. | *Morgen ist alles wieder in Ordnung.* |
| You win some, you lose some. | *Mal gewinnt man, mal verliert man.* |
| You can count yourself lucky. It could have been worse. | *Du kannst von Glück reden. Es hätte schlimmer kommen können.* |
| Don't lose heart! | *Verliere die Hoffnung nicht.* |
| Keep a stiff upper lip! | *Lass dir nichts anmerken!* |
| Keep your hair on! | *Rege dich nicht auf!* |
| Where there's life, there's hope. | *Wo Leben ist, ist Hoffnung.* |
| You have a fighting chance. | *Du hast eine reelle Chance.* |
| pin one's faith / hopes on something | *seinen ganzen Glauben / Hoffnung in etwas setzen* |
| escape death by the skin of one's teeth | *dem Tod mit knapper Not entkommen* |
| hang on by the skin of his teeth | *mit knapper Not etwas schaffen* |
| come within an ace of losing one's life | *dem Tod nur knapp entrinnen* |
| thank one's lucky stars that ... | *von Glück sagen können, dass ...* |
| come out of it unscathed / in one piece | *mit heiler Haut davonkommen* |
| get off lightly | *noch mal mit heiler Haut / mit dem Schrecken davonkommen* |
| take the rough with the smooth | *die Dinge nehmen, wie sie kommen* |
| scrape through an exam | *eine Prüfung mit Ach und Krach bestehen* |
| have one's up and downs | *seine Höhen und Tiefen haben* |

## QUICK CHECK 8: What's the *woggle*?

Ron discusses the financial situation with Michael, his tax advisor:

**R:** I'm still hanging on by *the skin of my woggle*. But it's not easy.
**M:** As we say in Munich, "where there's beer, there's hope". *You have to take the rough with the woggle.*
**R:** It's easy for you to say that, but I've been taking the rough with the rough for too long.
**M:** *Every cloud has a silver woggle.*
**R:** But it's nothing but rain and storms at the moment.

## DOUBLE CHECK 9: Body idioms

In den folgenden Idioms geht es um

*Knochen, Finger, Fuß, Herz, Gesicht, Nase, Mund und Zahn*

1. I can feel it in my ..........................
2. Don't let the opportunity slip right through your .......................... .
3. That's easy when you're born with a silver spoon in your ................ .
4. Try to always land on your .......................... .
5. Keep your .......................... crossed for me, mother!
6. Keep your .......................... up!
7. Put a bold .......................... on it!
8. Keep your .......................... on!
9. He escaped by skin of his .......................... .
10. Don't lose ..........................!

### TIME FOR A SMILE

Dear Reader's Digest,
We hardly know each other, yet I have been selected from so many millions to enter your free contest in which I may win £25,000. You have made me very happy.
Yours sincerely, *Miles*

# Love and friendship, and more

## *Liebe, Freundschaft und mehr*

11

**BIRD'S EYE VIEW**

### LEVEL I

1. *Freundschaft schließen* – Making friends
2. *Sich verlieben* – Falling in love

### LEVEL II

1. Friendship – *Freundschaft*
2. Affection – *Zuneigung*
3. Flirtation – *Flirten*
4. Is it love? – *Ist es Liebe?*

**TIME FOR A SMILE**

TO: Boss FROM: Blondie

RE: Changing Calendars from Y to K

I hope that I haven't misunderstood your instructions because none of this Y to K problem made much sense to me. At any rate, I have finished the changes on all of the company calendars for next year. The calendars have returned from the printer and are ready to be distributed with the following new months:
Januark - Februark - Mak - Julk.
I also changed all the days of each week to:
Sundak - Mondak - Tuesdak - Wednesdak etc.

Have a nice dak!

LEVEL 1

11

**Friendship is ...**

... when you can rely on a person to help you when you are in need. Of course, the people you can trust most are your bosom friends. If you are lucky there's always someone around to give you a hand.

**Love is ...**

... when you don't know whether you are coming or going. Some people call it being love sick. You want to be with one special person. It's something you can't really control. And when it goes wrong you feel like you've got a stone in your stomach.

## 1. *Freundschaft schließen* – Making friends

| | |
|---|---|
| *jemanden treffen / kennen lernen* | We met at Frank's dinner party two years ago. |
| *vorgestellt werden* | The lady of the house introduced us to each other. |
| *jemanden sympathisch finden* | I found her very nice to spend my leisure time with. |
| *näher kennen lernen* | I got to know her better after she had drunk a few beers. |
| *jemandem gefallen* | She was my type and I fancied her a lot. |
| *Freundschaft schließen* | We became good friends. Then she met Tony. |
| *jemandes Busenfreund sein* | Actually, Tony is not my bosom friend. |
| *dicke Freunde sein* | We weren't exactly the best of friends, but never mind. |
| *der beste Freund des Menschen* | Only the dog is a man's best friend. |
| *sich gut verstehen* | However, we got on quite well together. |
| *jemandem ein guter Freund sein* | He has been a good friend to me ever since I first met him. |
| *ein Freund in der Not* | He is a real friend who's there when you need him. |
| *jemanden zum Freund haben* | Having a friend in Tony helped me to survive a crisis. |

11

| | |
|---|---|
| *jemandem einen Freundschaftsdienst erweisen* | Once Tony did me a good turn. He let me have his car for a holiday. |
| *sich anfreunden mit* | Tony seems to make friends with the whole town. |
| *sich viele Freunde machen* | His helpfulness has won / made him a lot of friends. |
| *auf freundschaftlichem Fuße stehen mit jemandem* | He's on friendly terms even with the traffic wardens. |
| *freundschaftlich auseinander gehen* | When Tony's wife divorced him they parted as friends / on friendly terms. |
| *etwas gemeinsam haben mit* | I have a lot in common with Tony. |
| *gut Freund sein mit* | I'm also good friends with his wife, which makes problems. |
| *einen großen Freundeskreis haben* | She has a wide circle of friends. |
| *zur Hand gehen; behilflich sein* | Tony was always willing to give / lend me a hand. |
| *mit jemandem befreundet sein* | Ron is friends with Bob though he is a difficult old bastard. |

## QUICK CHECK 1: Typical German

Can you correct the mistakes?

1. We met us at Frank's dinner party two years ago.
2. I'm also good friend with his wife, which makes problems.
3. I learned to know her better after she had drunk a few beers.
4. His wife divorced herself from Tony but they parted as friends.

## QUICK CHECK 2: Those nasty little words

1. I'm good friends .......................... Tony's wife.
2. We weren't exactly the best .......................... friends.
3. When she divorced him they parted .......................... friends.
4. He's still on friendly terms .......................... her.
5. Having a friend .......................... Tony helped me to survive a crisis.

## 2. *Sich verlieben* – Falling in love

| | |
|---|---|
| *sich in jemanden verknallen* | My son, Tom, got carried away by Yvette, our new au-pair girl. |
| *verrückt sein nach* | He's absolutely crazy about her. |
| *verehren, anbeten* | And Yvette really seems to adore Tom. |
| *bewundern* | What he admires about Yvette is her smile. |
| *sich gut verstehen mit* | My wife and Yvette are getting on well with each other. |
| *sich verlieben* | I must say it's difficult not to fall in love with Yvette. |
| *einen Heiratsantrag machen* | Tom proposed to Yvette yesterday. |
| *sich verloben* | They are getting engaged on Tuesday. |
| *volljährig werden* | Tom has come of age but he's too young to start a family. |
| *um jemandes Hand anhalten* | Tom asked for Yvette's hand in marriage. |
| *Junggeselle sein* | Jill's brothers are not married, they are still bachelors. |
| *bis über beide Ohren verliebt sein* | They've only just met, but John's head over heels in love with her. |
| *strahlende / verliebte Augen haben* | The sun shines out of her eyes. |
| *im siebten Himmel sein / schweben* | He feels like he's walking on air since he met Yvette. |
| *sich vor Sehnsucht verzehren* | He's completely love-sick for her. |

### TIME FOR A SMILE

After Bill Gates' wedding night, his wife finally knew why he called his company Microsoft.

## QUICK CHECK 3: What's the *woggle*?

1. My son, Tom, *got woggled away by* Yvette, our new au-pair girl.
2. He's absolutely *woggly about* the girl.
3. He feels like he's *woggling on air* since he met Yvette.
4. Tom *woggled to* Yvette yesterday. They are *getting woggled* on Tuesday.

## QUICK CHECK 4: Body idioms

1. Tony was always willing to give me a .......................... .
2. Tom asked for Yvette's .......................... in marriage.
3. John's .......................... over .......................... in love with her.

### TIME FOR A SMILE

Do you know how to tell if a man is married? Watch him when he is driving a car, with a woman beside him. If he drives with both hands on the wheel, he's married.

## LEVEL 11

Birds of a feather flock together. You're judged by the type of people you *hobnob with.* If you *hang out with* suspicious characters, you will be regarded as suspicious yourself. Of course, it's not so easy to find the right people to *keep company with.* You think you've got someone to trust and then you notice he's only a *fair-weather friend*, and you certainly notice it too late.

### 1. Friendship – *Freundschaft*

| | |
|---|---|
| break the ice | *das Eis brechen; einen Durchbruch erzielen* |
| be hail-fellow-well-met with someone | *jemanden kumpelhaft behandeln* |
| be in someone's good books / favours | *bei jemandem einen Stein im Brett haben* |
| be in someone's good graces | *in jemandes Gunst stehen* |
| put in a good word for someone | *ein gutes Wort für jemanden einlegen* |
| get a pat on the back | *ein Lob bekommen* |
| pull strings | *seine Beziehungen spielen lassen* |
| take sides with someone | *für jemanden Partei ergreifen; sich auf jemandes Seite schlagen* |
| keep track of | *nicht aus den Augen verlieren* |
| strike up a friendship | *sich anfreunden; eine Freundschaft anfangen* |
| hobnob with someone | *mit jemandem freundschaftlich verkehren* |
| rub shoulders with someone | *mit jemandem auf Du und Du sein* |
| be someone after one's own heart | *ganz nach jemandes Geschmack / Herzen sein* |
| be well-disposed towards someone | *jemandem wohlgesinnt sein* |
| be close to someone | *jemandem nahe stehen* |
| come out of one's shell | *aus sich herausgehen* |
| hang out / around with someone | *seine Freizeit mit jemandem verbringen* |

| | |
|---|---|
| keep someone company | *jemandem Gesellschaft leisten* |
| be on good terms with | *auf gutem Fuß stehen mit* |
| pal up /around with someone | *sich mit jemandem anfreunden* |
| go through hell and high water for someone | *für jemanden durchs Feuer gehen* |
| be (as) thick as thieves | *wie Pech und Schwefel zusammenhalten* |
| be hand in glove; be in cahoots / league | *unter einer Decke stecken* |
| get on like a house on fire | *hervorragend miteinander auskommen* |
| cosy up to someone | *sich bei jemandem einschmeicheln* |
| curry favour with someone | *sich bei jemandem lieb Kind machen* |
| use the old-boys' network | *seine Beziehungen spielen lassen* |
| be a fair-weather friend | *nur in guten Zeiten ein Freund sein* |
| A friend in need is a friend indeed. | *Wahre Freunde zeigen sich in der Not.* |

## QUICK CHECK 5: Idioms with a p

1. The new boss is *p_ _ _ing up with* his female employees.
2. She deserves a *p_ _ on the back* for all the hard work she's done.
3. Would you please *p_ _ in a good word for* me with the boss?
4. You have to *p_ _ _ strings* if you want to be successful in business.

## QUICK CHECK 6: What a mess!

Can you put the words in *italics* back to where they belong?

Jane and Sarah about their long-standing friendship:

**S:** We've known each other a long time. How long have we been *getting* out together?

**J:** More than ten years. And we've been *hanging* on like a house on fire.

**S:** Right, but now we've got a problem. I think you've been *currying* up to my boyfriend.

**J:** It's the other way round. He's *cosying* favour with me.

TIME FOR A SMILE

A boss tells his new employee, "I'll give you eight bucks an hour starting today and in three months I'll raise it to ten bucks an hour. So when would you like to start?"
"In three months."

## 2. Affection – *Zuneigung*

| | |
|---|---|
| meet a kindred spirit / soul mate | *einer verwandten Seele begegnen* |
| warm the cockles of someone's heart | *jemandes Herz erwärmen* |
| warm up to someone | *mit jemandem warm werden* |
| hit it off with someone | *sich mit jemandem verstehen* |
| have one's eye on someone | *ein Auge haben auf jemanden* |
| have a soft spot / weakness for someone | *eine Schwäche für jemanden haben* |
| take a fancy / liking / shine to someone | *sich für jemanden interessieren; einen Narren an jemandem fressen* |
| carry a torch for someone | *nach jemandem schmachten* |
| only have eyes for someone | *nur für einen Augen haben* |

## 3. Flirtation – *Flirten*

| | |
|---|---|
| court a woman | *einer Frau den Hof machen* |
| make a pass | *einen Annäherungsversuch machen* |
| make eyes at someone | *jemandem schöne Augen machen* |
| give someone the glad eye | *jemandem schöne Augen machen* |
| make sheep's eyes at someone | *jemandem verliebte Blicke zuwerfen* |
| play hard to get | *sich zieren* |
| whisper sweet nothings | *Süßholz raspeln* |
| turn on the old charm | *seinen Charme spielen lassen* |
| play footsie with someone | *mit jemandem (unter dem Tisch) füßeln* |
| pick someone up | *jemanden aufreißen* |
| fling one's arms around someone's neck | *jemandem um den Hals fallen* |

| | |
|---|---|
| shack up with someone | *mit jemandem zusammenziehen* |
| wait on someone hand and foot | *jemanden auf Händen tragen* |
| be in heat | *heiß sein; angetörnt sein* |
| go all the way | *das Ding bis zum Ende durchziehen* |
| bed down with someone; get into the sack with someone; sack down with someone | *mit jemandem in die Kiste springen / ins Bett gehen* |
| get a leg over someone | *jemanden ins Bett kriegen* |
| I wouldn't throw him / her out of bed. | *Ihn / Sie würde ich nicht von der Bettkante schubsen.* |
| I'd drink her bathwater. | *Ich würde ihr Badewasser schlürfen.* |
| undress someone with one's eyes | *jemanden mit den Augen ausziehen* |

## QUICK CHECK 7: Remember the idioms?

| | |
|---|---|
| touch his / her feet lightly with one's own feet under a table, as an expression of sexual interest | .................... |
| live together when not married | .................... |
| look at someone in a loving but foolish way | .................... |
| make oneself seem more attractive by not immediately accepting an invitation | .................... |

## QUICK CHECK 8: Going all the way

Frank discusses his new girlfriend with Ron:

**R:** So you've *made a* .......................... *at* Maria?

**F:** Not really, but I guess I .......................... *on the old charm* a bit. You've got to do your best, you know.

**R:** My God, Frank, you're unbelievable. You .......................... *someone up* and you're always successful. Do you really like her?

**F:** Well, to tell you the truth, *I could drink her* .......................... .

**R:** Frank, you're an M.C.P. (Male Chauvinist Pig).

## 4. Is it love? – *Ist es Liebe?*

| | |
|---|---|
| be sweet on someone; go soft on someone | *in jemanden verknallt sein* |
| fall for someone; go a bundle on someone | *sich in jemanden verknallen* |
| have a crush on someone | *in jemanden verknallt / verliebt / vernarrt sein* |
| have a thing going with someone | *mit jemandem etwas am Laufen haben* |
| turn someone's head | *jemandem den Kopf verdrehen* |
| love at first sight | *Liebe auf den ersten Blick* |
| hook / land oneself a millionaire | *sich einen Millionär angeln* |
| be wild / crazy / mad / nuts about someone | *verrückt nach jemandem sein* |
| be hooked /stuck on someone | *in jemanden vernarrt sein* |
| be the apple of someone's eye | *jemandes Augapfel sein* |
| He thinks life's a bed of roses. | *Bei ihm hängt der Himmel voller Geigen.* |
| be walking on air | *im sieb(en)ten Himmel sein* |

## QUICK CHECK 10: Take a vowel for a heart

Tom told me he's g❤n❤ a b❤ndl❤ on Lara, a young girl from Poland. He said he's never met anyone like that and he was completely h❤❤k❤d on her. Well, Tom always was a bit impressionable; he's so young! But in a way he's a bit naïve. He thinks life is a b❤d of r❤s❤s and doesn't see that some people are down in the dumps. Anyway, never mind, he's w❤lk❤ng on ❤❤r, at least for the time being.

11

## QUICK CHECK 11: Body idioms

Where do these parts of the body go?

| | | |
|---|---|---|
| foot | back | hand (2x) |
| shoulders | heart | eye |

1. "Well done!" he said and patted him on the __________.
2. Tom tries to rub __________ with the rich people of the town.
3. I found him to be __________ in glove with my worst enemy.
4. He is a boy after my own __________.
5. Have you noticed, Tim is giving Sue the glad __________?
6. He seems to expect to be waited on __________ and __________.

### TIME FOR A SMILE

Lem: "I got fired from my job as a bank guard."
Clem: "That's awful. What happened?"
Lem: "Well a thief came in to rob a bank. I drew my gun. I told him that if he took one more step, I'd let him have it."
Clem: "What did the thief do then?"
Lem: "He took one more step so I let him have it. I didn't want that stupid gun anyhow!"

# Managing conflicts

## *Umgang mit Konflikten*

12

### Bird's eye view

**LEVEL I**

1. *Sich nicht riechen können* – Not stand the sight of someone
2. *Schimpfen und beleidigen* – Moaning and insulting
3. *Betrügen und belügen* – Deceiving and lying
4. *Handgreiflich werden* – Coming to blows

**LEVEL II**

1. Like cat and dog – *Wie Hund und Katz*
2. How to be nasty – *Die Kunst, ekelhaft zu sein*
3. Insulting and getting insulted – *Beleidigen und beleidigt sein*
4. Coming to blows – *Handgreiflich werden*
5. Making (it) up again – *Sich wieder vertragen*

### Time for a smile

*How to be nasty*

You're not the sharpest knife in our drawer.
You've got a room temperature IQ.
If brains were taxed, you'd get a rebate.
You're about as bright as Alaska in December.
Did you type these with your feet?
I asked for a letter, not your dirty fingerprints.

## LEVEL 1

Sometimes you meet people you disapprove of the very first time you meet them. It's a matter of chemistry. You have a built-in aversion to them. There's nothing you can do about it. Then again you may also encounter characters who are simply bad. They feel no guilt when lying and cheating and deceiving other people. Very often these types can be very physical, coming to blows over the smallest problems. It's better to avoid them if possible.

### 1. *Sich nicht riechen können* – Not stand the sight of someone

| | |
|---|---|
| *nicht jemandes Fall sein* | Your Honour, when I first saw Sue's boyfriend Bill I knew he was not exactly my type. |
| *nicht mögen* | I didn't like the looks of this man. |
| *Abneigung auf den ersten Blick* | It was dislike from the first minute. |
| *einen schlechten Eindruck bekommen von* | First impressions are often wrong, but I got a bad impression of Bill. |
| *nicht scharf sein auf* | So I wasn't very keen on his hanging around the house. |
| *nicht mögen* | It wasn't only his green hair which I disliked. |
| *missbilligen* | I also disapproved of his table manners. He didn't have any. |
| *anstößig finden* | What I found particularly objectionable in Bill was his foul language. |
| *eine Abneigung haben vor* | And I have an aversion to all these four-letter words. |
| *es nicht vertragen können* | I love classical music and I couldn't stand their heavy metal records. |
| *ablehnen; missbilligen* | So I deeply disapproved of Sue's friendship with Bill. |
| *nicht ausstehen können* | But it's not just a question of taste. Bill was not honest and I loathe liars. |

| | |
|---|---|
| *verachten* | I hate liars. That's why I detest most politicians. |
| *verabscheuen* | Bill was a member of the Hell Angels and I abhor violence. |
| *empören; mit Abscheu erfüllen; abstoßen* | The violent films Bill and Sue watched all the time revolted me. |
| *nicht ertragen können* | I couldn't bear the way he treated animals. |
| *angewidert sein* | I was shocked and disgusted when he kicked our dog. And that was the last straw. |
| *hassen* | Your Honour will now understand that I hated this person and that I had to find a solution. |

## QUICK CHECK 1: Which one is wrong?

**1.** etwas nicht ertragen können

**A.** I *can't bear* the way he treated animals.
**B.** I *can't stand* their heavy metal records.
**C.** I *can't support* my family.
**D.** I *can't tolerate* your foul language.

**2.** etwas nicht mögen

**A.** You may *disagree,* but that's what I think.
**B.** I *wasn't very keen on* his marrying my daughter.
**C.** I *dislike* his looks.
**D.** I *disapprove* of his manners.

**3.** etwas / jemanden verabscheuen

**A.** Bill was not honest and I *loathe* liars.
**B.** I *have an aversion* to all four-letter words.
**C.** I *abhor* cowards.
**D.** I *object to* all forms of violence.

### TIME FOR A SMILE

***How to be insulting***

Are you really that bald or is your neck just blowing a bubble?

"You remind me of a famous movie star." –
"Really? Which one?" – "Lassie."

## 2. *Schimpfen und beleidigen* – Moaning and insulting

| | |
|---|---|
| *zutiefst beleidigt* | My wife is often deeply offended. Then she refuses to speak to me. This is one of our typical dialogues. |
| *ein beleidigtes Gesicht machen* | Darling you look hurt. What's the matter? |
| *jemanden verletzen* | Did I offend you in some way? |
| *jemandes Gefühle verletzen* | Tell me if I hurt your feelings, Darling. |
| *jemanden nicht beleidigen wollen* | I didn't mean any offence when I said that I like my mother's strawberry cakes. |
| *zimperlich sein* | Don't make such a fuss! |
| *jemanden anschreien* | Please don't shout at me! |
| *ein taktloser Mensch sein* | You think I have no sense of tact. |
| *etwas in den falschen Hals bekommen* | You took it the wrong way when I said you should go to a beauty farm from time to time. |
| *taktlos sein* | I didn't mean to be tactless. I wanted to offer you a holiday on that farm. |
| *unter der Gürtellinie* | By the way, your remarks about my appearance are also below the belt. |
| *beleidigend werden* | Don't start insulting me. |
| *Wer im Glashaus sitzt, soll nicht mit Steinen werfen.* | People in glass houses shouldn't throw stones. |
| *Beleidigungsklage einreichen / anstrengen* | By the way, our best friend, Cathy, has started a libel suit against you. |
| *sich Beleidigungen an den Kopf werfen* | You and Cathy are always trading insults. |
| *zutiefst verletzt sein* | Cathy is deeply hurt, her husband told me. |
| *durch den Dreck ziehen* | He said you dragged Cathy through the mud. |
| *mit Dreck bewerfen* | You said Cathy looked like the back of a bus. Stop slinging mud at people. |
| *jemanden wie den letzten Dreck behandeln* | You treat everybody like dirt, including me. |
| *empfindlich sein* | You have no reason to be so sensitive when I mention beauty farms. |

## QUICK CHECK 2: Beef up your word power

What's the corresponding noun?

| | |
|---|---|
| 1. You deeply *offended* me. | I didn't mean any ......................... . |
| 2. Don't start *insulting* me. | It wasn't an ........................., it was a compliment. |
| 3. I was *disgusted* with the way you behaved towards Anne. | Why should my behaviour fill you with ......................... . |

## 3. *Betrügen und belügen* – Deceiving and lying

| | |
|---|---|
| *unehrlich sein* | I knew Phil was dishonest the first time we met. |
| *es mit der Wahrheit nicht so genau nehmen* | He treats the truth lightly. |
| *der Wahrheit aus dem Weg gehen* | Actually, he really avoids the truth. |
| *schummeln / jemanden beschummeln* | He's always trying to cheat people. |
| *beschwindeln* | He'll swindle you where he can. |
| *zu Notlügen greifen* | He lies, and they're not just white lies. |
| *lügen / jemanden belügen* | Phil tells lies to cause trouble for people. |
| *Lügen auftischen* | He dishes out lies as if it were the most natural thing in the world. |
| *jemanden reinlegen* | He hoodwinked us about his teaching skills. |
| *Geld unterschlagen* | Eventually he was caught for embezzling money. |
| *Schecks fälschen* | The police said he had falsified a lot of cheques. |
| *betrügen* | In his private life he deceived his wife. |
| *jemanden um sein Geld bringen* | And of course, he also cheated the tax office out of money. |

## QUICK CHECK 3: Letter mix-up

Do you see the mistakes?

1. He's always trying to teach people.
2. He always deveiced his wife.
3. He streat the truth lightly.

## 4. Handgreiflich werden – *Coming to blows*

| | |
|---|---|
| *jemanden schubsen* | A man gave me a shove at the bus stop. |
| *jemanden einen Schubs geben* | Of course, I gave him a push back. |
| *jemanden anrempeln* | Then two other people jostled me on the way to the bus. |
| *jemandem einen Stoß versetzen* | Well, I gave one of them a prod. |
| *jemanden schlagen* | And he tried to hit me. |
| *jemandem eine Ohrfeige geben* | I was so cross. I moved next to him and gave him a box on the ears. |
| *jemanden ohrfeigen* | I know boxing someone's ears is not very civilized. |
| *jemanden einen Rippenstoß versetzen* | Before I knew what was happening he had poked me in the ribs. |
| *jemandem eins auf die Nase geben* | That was it. I punched his nose. |
| *jemanden unter die Gürtellinie schlagen* | He was an unfair lout and hit me below the belt. |
| *jemandem eine Abreibung verpassen* | I lost my temper and gave him a thrashing. |
| *jemanden verprügeln* | I really beat him up in fact. |
| *jemandem eine Tracht Prügel geben* | He got a really good hiding. |
| *jemanden zusammenschlagen* | I beat him to a pulp. |
| *jemanden niederschlagen* | He was knocked down and didn't get up again. |
| *jemanden k. o. schlagen* | I'd really knocked him out. |
| *jemandem einen Fußtritt geben* | I didn't actually kick him when he was down, but the police didn't believe me anyway. |

### QUICK CHECK 4: Phrases with a p

1. I gave one of them a *p*_ _ _.
2. He *p*_ _ _ _ _ _ my nose.
3. Then I beat him to a *p*_ _ _ .

## LEVEL ⓜ

I don't want to say it's healthy but actually I *hate some people's guts.* It's the person or people who just work according to figures and don't take into account our years of good work and cooperation with their company. Their company is bigger than ours so they just *ride roughshod over* us. They've cancelled out contracts because they are in a panic. Anyhow they've certainly *pulled the rug from under our feet.* I never believed they would *go overboard* in this way. It shows how wrong you can be.

### TIME FOR A SMILE

***How to be insulting***
Last time I saw a face like yours
I fed it a banana.

## 1. Like cat and dog – *Wie Hund und Katz*

| | |
|---|---|
| He's not my kettle of fish. | *Er ist nicht mein Typ.* |
| He's not my cup of tea. | *Er ist nicht mein Fall.* |
| be on bad terms with | *sich nicht gut mit jemandem verstehen* |
| give someone the cold shoulder | *jemandem die kalte Schulter zeigen* |
| not stomach someone | *jemanden nicht ausstehen können* |
| send someone to Coventry | *jemanden schneiden* |
| be fed up with someone | *genug von jemandem haben* |
| give a wide berth to someone | *einen großen Bogen um jemanden machen* |
| turn someone off | *jemanden anwidern* |
| not touch someone with a bargepole | *jemanden nicht einmal mit der Kohlenzange anfassen* |

| | |
|---|---|
| have it in for someone | *jemanden auf dem Kieker haben* |
| be an awkward customer | *ein unangenehmer Zeitgenosse sein* |
| be a nasty piece of work | *ein widerlicher Mensch sein* |
| He really gets on my wick. | *Er geht mir auf den Geist.* |
| be a pain in the ass (sl) | *auf den Sack gehen* |
| not stand someone | *jemanden nicht ausstehen können* |
| He turns my stomach. | *Es dreht mir den Magen um, wenn ich ihn sehe.* |
| set one's teeth on edge | *jemandem auf die Nerven gehen* |
| be at loggerheads with someone | *sich mit jemandem in den Haaren liegen* |
| ride roughshod over someone | *jemanden rücksichtslos behandeln; schikanieren* |
| send a shiver up one's spine | *jemanden eine Gänsehaut über den Rücken jagen* |
| be gunning for someone | *jemanden im Visier haben* |
| stick a knife in someone's back | *jemandem den Dolchstoß versetzen; jemandem in den Rücken fallen* |
| have a bone to pick with someone | *mit jemandem ein Hühnchen zu rupfen haben* |
| get even with someone | *mit jemandem abrechnen; sich rächen* |
| There's no love lost between them. | *Sie können sich nicht leiden.* |
| Don't bite the hand that feeds you. | *Man sollte nicht die Hand beißen, die einen füttert.* |

## TIME FOR A SMILE

Groucho Marx hated the meaningless phrases that pepper business letters. Once, having received a letter from his bank manager with the standard ending, "If I can be of any service to you, please do not hesitate to call on me," he wrote back:

Dear Sir,
The best thing you can do to be of service to me is to steal some money from the account of one of your richer clients and credit it to mine.

## QUICK CHECK 5: Fill them in

Nine words to help you complete three idioms.

| verbs | nouns |
|---|---|
| | knife |
| stick | bone |
| set | back |
| have got | teeth |
| pick | edge |

1. I'm very disappointed. I have always trusted him and now he's trying to ................ *a* ................ *in my* ................ .
2. I ................ *a* ................*to* ................ *with you.* Where's the money I left on the kitchen table?
3. Doesn't he make you feel physically uncomfortable? – He ................ *my* ................ *on* ................ as soon as he enters the room.

## QUICK CHECK 6: What's it in English?

Jean and Tony discuss their friend Liz:

J: I really don't know what's wrong. I met Liz yesterday and I got the feeling (*sie hat mich auf dem Kieker*).

T: What have you done to her? Maybe she wants to (*sich an dir rächen*) for something you've done.

J: I can't remember anything. Maybe it's something I said.

T: Yes, you're sometimes a bit tactless. But I must say Liz is (*eine unangenehme Zeitgenossin*), too.

J: Well, there's certainly (*wir können uns nicht leiden*).

## 2. How to be nasty – *Die Kunst, ekelhaft zu sein*

| | |
|---|---|
| laugh up one's sleeve | *heimliche Schadenfreude empfinden* |
| look daggers at someone | *mit Blicken töten* |
| run someone down behind his back | *jemanden hinter seinem Rücken schlecht machen* |

| | |
|---|---|
| give someone a black look | *jemandem einen finsteren Blick zuwerfen* |
| give someone a dirty look | *jemandem einen verächtlichen Blick zuwerfen* |
| cut the ground from under someone | *jemandem den Boden unter den Füßen wegziehen* |
| pull the rug / carpet from under someone's feet | *jemandem den Boden unter den Füßen wegziehen* |
| pour cold water on someone's plans | *jemandem einen Strich durch die Rechnung machen* |
| shoot someone's plans down | *jemandes Pläne durchkreuzen* |
| throw / put a spanner in the works; put a spoke into someone's wheel | *Sand ins Getriebe streuen; jemandem Knüppel zwischen die Beine werfen* |
| blow the whistle on someone / something | *jemanden / etwas auffliegen lassen* |
| get one's knife into someone | *es auf jemanden abgesehen haben; jemanden heftig kritisieren* |
| treat someone like a leper | *jemanden wie einen Aussätzigen behandeln* |
| have someone under one's thumb | *jemanden unter seiner Fuchtel haben* |
| even / settle the score | *eine Rechnung begleichen* |
| give someone short shrift | *kurzen Prozess mit jemandem machen* |
| be up to no good | *nichts Gutes im Schilde führen* |
| settle an old score | *eine offene Rechnung begleichen* |
| hassle someone | *jemanden schikanieren / nerven* |
| do it in cold blood | *etwas kaltblütig / aus purer Berechnung tun* |
| have someone over a barrel | *jemanden in der Zange haben* |
| get someone's goat | *jemanden auf die Palme bringen* |
| drive someone up the wall | *jemanden wahnsinnig / verrückt machen* |
| slag someone off | *über jemanden herziehen; jemanden madig machen* |

## QUICK CHECK 7: It's your choice again

1. Ron is completely under Anne's control: She's got him under her **A.** thumb / **B.** finger / **C.** foot.
2. The way she acts makes it difficult for him to proceed with the project. She is cutting **A.** the ground / **B.** the grass / **C.** the carpet from under his feet.
3. She knew all along that Ron had a girlfriend and was laughing up **A.** her fist / **B.** thumb / **C.** her sleeve at Ron.

## QUICK CHECK 8: What's the *woggle*?

Ron and Bryan talk about Peter whom they've just met in the pub.

**R:** Well, Pete's not changed much. He's still *woggling people off* behind their backs.

**B:** You're right there. He's always *got his woggle into someone* or another.

**R:** One of these days somebody will get to know what he's saying and then they'll *woggle the score* with him. And it'll serve him right.

## 3. Insulting and getting insulted – *Beleidigen und beleidigt sein*

| | |
|---|---|
| jump down someone's throat | *jemanden anschnauzen* |
| ruffle someone's feathers | *jemanden verärgern; jemanden gegen den Strich bürsten* |
| put one's foot in it / one's mouth | *ins Fettnäpfchen treten; einen Bock schießen* |
| throw the book at someone | *jemandem gehörig den Kopf waschen* |
| add insult to injury | *einer Kränkung eine Beleidigung draufsatteln* |
| swear like a trooper | *wie ein Bierkutscher fluchen* |
| cut someone to the bone | *jemanden zutiefst verletzen* |
| force something down someone's throat | *jemandem etwas mit allen Mitteln einreden wollen* |
| give the finger to someone. | *jemandem den (Effenberg-)Stinkefinger zeigen* |

| | |
|---|---|
| call someone names | *jemanden beschimpfen* |
| put someone's nose out of joint | *jemanden schwer beleidigen* |
| thumb one's nose at someone | *jemandem eine lange Nase machen* |
| go off half-cocked | *überreagieren; wütend werden* |
| go off in a huff | *eingeschnappt sein; beleidigt abziehen* |
| not have all one's marbles | *nicht mehr alle Tassen im Schrank haben* |
| be as nutty as a fruitcake | *völlig verrückt / übergeschnappt sein* |
| have a screw loose | *eine Schraube locker haben; nicht alle Tassen im Schrank haben* |
| have bats in the belfry | *eine Meise haben* |
| That's a load of bullshit! | *Nichts als Schwachsinn!* |
| Climb a tree! | *Hau ab!; Verschwinde!* |
| Go fly a kite! | *Verschwinde! / Zieh Leine!* |
| Go and take a running jump! | *Geh und verzieh dich!* |
| It's no skin off my ass / nose. | *Das ist mir egal. Das geht mir am Arsch vorbei.* |

### TIME FOR A SMILE

A man walked into a lawyer's office and inquired about the rates.
"Fifty dollars for three questions," replied the lawyer.
"Isn't that awfully steep?" asked the man.
"Yes," the lawyer replied, "and what was your third question?"

## QUICK CHECK 9: Body idioms

Five are wrong – only three are right.

| | | | |
|---|---|---|---|
| mouth | nose | teeth | bone |
| heart | throat | stomach | ass |

1. Stop being so critical. You always cut down Anita to the .................................. .
2. You're always hurting everybody's feelings. Be more reserved and don't put Anita's .................................. out of joint all the time.
3. And stop telling everybody how you would run the country. Nobody likes having your extremist ideas forced down their .......................... .

## 4. Coming to blows – *Handgreiflich werden*

| | |
|---|---|
| cut up rough | *Krach schlagen; stürmisch / gewalttätig werden* |
| get hot under the collar; get hot and bothered | *sich aufregen; wütend werden* |
| give someone hell | *jemandem die Hölle heiß machen* |
| fight fire with fire | *Gleiches mit Gleichem vergelten* |
| go off the deep end | *außer sich geraten* |
| have a barney / argy-bargy | *einen lautstarken Krach / Streit haben* |
| take someone to task (about something) | *sich jemanden vorknöpfen / kaufen* |
| fight someone tooth and nail | *jemanden mit Zähnen und Klauen bekämpfen* |
| go at it hammer and tongs | *sich streiten, dass die Fetzen fliegen* |
| come to blows (over) | *handgreiflich werden; sich in die Haare geraten* |
| give someone a good hiding | *jemandem die Hucke voll hauen* |
| put someone's face / nose out of joint (sl) | *jemandem die Fresse polieren* |
| beat someone up / clobber someone | *jemanden aufmischen / verprügeln* |
| beat someone black and blue | *jemanden grün und blau / windelweich schlagen* |
| give someone a black eye | *jemandem ein blaues Auge verpassen* |
| knock the spots off someone | *jemanden heftig verprügeln / besiegen* |
| be at each other's throats | *sich gegenseitig an den Kragen gehen* |
| beat / knock the living daylights / the stuffing out of someone | *jemanden windelweich schlagen* |
| cook someone's goose | *jemandem den Garaus machen* |
| give someone a licking | *jemandem eine ordentliche Abreibung verpassen* |
| Them's fighting words. | *Du willst wohl Streit anfangen?* |
| mess someone up | *jemanden verprügeln* |
| have a free-for-all | *ein wildes Gerangel haben* |
| point a gun at someone's head | *jemandem das Messer an die Kehle setzen* |
| do someone in (sl) | *jemanden um die Ecke bringen* |
| blow someone away (sl) | *jemanden um die Ecke bringen* |
| Not over my dead body! | *Nur über meine Leiche!* |

## QUICK CHECK 10: Let's go *woggling* again

Bryan has drunk too much. Bryan, Ron and Sid:

**R:** Hey, don't shout so loud. People are looking.
**B:** I'll give him *a black woggle* if he keeps staring.
**R:** My God, you're drunk. Look, that big fellow's coming over. Watch out or we'll be *having a woggle.*
**B:** I couldn't care less. I'll *give him woggle* if he comes near me.
**S:** Hey, *them's woggling words.* Take your glasses off.

## 5. Making (it) up again – *Sich wieder vertragen*

| | |
|---|---|
| hold out the olive branch | *seinen Friedenswillen zeigen* |
| cool off | *sich abregen* |
| patch things up | *sich wieder vertragen* |
| eat one's words | *einen Irrtum eingestehen; etwas zurücknehmen* |
| get hold of the wrong end of the stick | *etwas in den falschen Hals bekommen* |
| a storm in a teacup | *ein Sturm im Wasserglas* |
| pour oil on troubled waters | *die Wogen glätten / beruhigen* |
| come to terms with a situation | *sich mit einer Situation abfinden* |
| have it out with someone | *mit jemandem offen sprechen* |
| put something straight | *etwas klar / in aller Deutlichkeit aussprechen* |
| bury the hatchet | *das Kriegsbeil begraben* |
| clear the air / atmosphere | *die Situation entschärfen* |
| be in the same boat | *im gleichen Boot sitzen* |
| eat dirt; eat humble pie | *seine Fehler einsehen und sich entschuldigen müssen; zu Kreuze kriechen* |
| Keep your shirt on!; Keep your hair on! | *Reg dich ab!; Nur ruhig Blut!* |
| No hard feelings! | *Nicht böse sein!; Das macht doch nichts!* |

## QUICK CHECK 11: More silly questions

You want to clear the air and patch things up so what will you

1. pour on troubled waters?
2. hold out to your partner?
3. bury?

## QUICK CHECK 12: A vowel for an x

Rob, Sid and Bryan. Rob intervenes to help Bryan in the pub:

**R:** Now then, Sid, you're *getting the wrxng xnd of the stxck.*
**S:** You must be joking. He was threatening me.
**R:** He's just a bit drunk. He's only *getting it xxt of his sxstxm.*
**S:** Let's *pxt something strxxght.* If he does that again, I'll bop him.

### TIME FOR A SMILE

The critic was telephoning in the review of a new play.
"Tell me," said the editor, "did it have a happy ending?"
"Yes," replied the critic. "Everyone was delighted when it was all over."

# The way we communicate

## *Wie wir miteinander reden*

13

BIRD'S EYE VIEW

### LEVEL 1

1. *So reden wir* – The way we say it
2. *Austausch von Informationen* – Exchanging information
3. *Lautstark werden* – Raising one's voice
4. *Aussagen machen* – Making statements

### LEVEL 2

1. Silence is golden – *Schweigen ist Gold*
2. Hearing and listening – *Hören und zuhören*
3. Losing and finding one's voice – *Seine Sprache verlieren und wiederfinden*
4. In strict confidence – *Ganz im Vertrauen*
5. Ways of saying it – *Der Ton macht die Musik*
6. Letting them know – *Informieren*
7. Avoiding the truth – *Der Wahrheit aus dem Wege gehen*
8. Gossips and gasbags – *Klatschbasen und Quasseltanten*

TIME FOR A SMILE

*To err is human.*

This'll be a short meeting.
Of course there's film in the camera.
Your table will be ready in five minutes.
You can put it together yourself in five minutes.
When it says empty, there's always a liter or two left.
Take off your clothes, the doctor will be with you in a minute.

## LEVEL 1

13

I met Jane on the street yesterday. She was telling me she'd been exaggerating in her professional life. She mentioned that she'd done overtime for a year and eventually she got ill. Actually she'd had a nervous breakdown. Her doctor convinced her to give up her job. I was trying to find out what she lives off. I think there must be money in her background.

### 1. *So reden wir* – The way we say it

| | |
|---|---|
| *mit jemandem sprechen wollen* | I saw Lydia at the party a few minutes ago and I wanted to speak to her. |
| *keine Antwort geben* | I said "hello" but she gave no reply. |
| *seine Lebensgeschichte erzählen* | I needed to tell her the story of my life. |
| *plaudern mit* | But she was chatting with some ladies about clothes and cooking. |
| *reden / sprechen über* | I think she doesn't want to talk about our future any more. |
| *ein Gespräch über ... mit jemandem haben* | Maybe it's because we had a long conversation about sexual matters a week ago. |
| *jemandem etwas vorwerfen* | I reproached her for being heartless and insensitive. |
| *ausdrücken* | I know I have difficulties to express my feelings in words. |
| *übertreiben* | She told me to stop exaggerating and that I was a neurotic. |
| *etwas nie wieder sagen* | Neurotic! I asked her never to say that again. |
| *eine Bemerkung machen über* | It wasn't the first time she had made indiscreet remarks about my relationship with women. |
| *aufhören zu reden* | Oh! Those ladies have stopped talking now. |
| *erklären* | I'll walk up to Lydia and explain my problems to her. |
| *mention* | Shall I mention that my aunt left me £10,000? |
| *eine Andeutung machen* | I'll just drop a hint that one of her prophecies has come true. |
| *schmeicheln* | That'll flatter her a lot. |

13

## QUICK CHECK 1: What a mess!

Can you rearrange the letters?

1. I was *attching* with some ladies.
2. I wanted to tell them the *rosty* of my *file.*
3. I need to *aplexin* my problems to them.
4. I'll *mointen* that I won at the horse races.
5. I'll just *prod* a *thin* that I'm a very rich man.

### TIME FOR A SMILE

She said to her husband the other day, "Have you got a good memory for faces?" He said yes, he did have a good memory for faces. She said, "That's just as well – I've just broken your shaving mirror."

## 2. *Austausch von Informationen* – Exchanging information

| | |
|---|---|
| *jemanden verhören* | Yesterday I was questioned by the police. |
| *eine Frage beantworten* | I had to answer all sorts of questions. |
| *sich erkundigen nach* | The police were inquiring about my new neighbour, Paul Balls. |
| *beschreiben* | Can you describe the gentleman, sir? |
| *eine genaue Beschreibung* | I'm afraid my description won't be very precise. I hardly knew the man. |
| *verstehen* | Sorry, I didn't catch his name. |
| *richtig aussprechen* | His name is Balls, but I'm not sure if I am pronouncing it correctly. |
| *langsamer wiederholen* | Could you repeat that more slowly, please? |
| *buchstabieren* | Would you be so kind as to spell it? Balls with double l or w? |
| *eine Frage stellen* | Double l. Now may I ask you a question for a change? |
| *empfehlen* | You said Balls was dangerous. What do you recommend me to do? |

| | |
|---|---|
| *ein Rat geben; raten* | Can you give me a good piece of advice? Would you advise me to change my hotel, for example? |
| *vorschlagen, dass* | Hotel? If you ask me, I suggest that you leave the city immediately. |
| *versprechen; ein Versprechen halten* | But the police promised to help me. You should keep your promise. |
| *jemanden unterrichten, informieren* | Well, we only promised to inform you after we have arrested Balls. |
| *gestehen, dass* | I must confess that I am a bit worried. |

## QUICK CHECK 2: Beef up your word power

Find the verb.

| noun | Verb |
|---|---|
| description | *describe* |
| repetition | ........... |
| advice | ........... |
| suggestion | ........... |
| promise | ........... |

## QUICK CHECK 3: Word power the other way round

| verb | Noun |
|---|---|
| inform | ........... |
| inquire | ........... |
| repeat | ........... |
| recommend | ........... |
| confess | ........... |

## 3. *Lautstark werden* – Raising one's voice

| | |
|---|---|
| *flüstern* | I could hear voices. Two men were whispering behind the bushes. |
| *streiten über* | I don't want to argue with you about money. |
| *streiten über* | Keep that 40 percent and stop quarrelling about it. Let's discuss it calmly. |
| *verlangen; fordern* | I demand 60 percent because it was my plan. |
| *eine Auseinandersetzung haben* | We had this argument before, didn't we? |
| *rufen; ein Ruf* | Suddenly I heard a call for help. It was one of the men who was calling for help. |
| *Wutschrei* | Then there were loud yells of rage. |
| *vor Schmerzen aufschreien* | And then one of the men cried out in pain. |
| *schreien; schimpfen; zurufen* | He appeared behind the bushes and shouted to me that I should call the police. |
| *Schmerzensschrei* | His screams of pain became fainter. Then there was silence. |

## QUICK CHECK 4: Ways of speaking

We give you a definition – you give us the verb.

1. say something in a loud voice: ..............................
2. express an opposite opinion; to exchange angry words: ............
3. speak or say something quietly, using only your breath, so that only the people closest to you can hear: ..........................

## QUICK CHECK 5: A letter mix to sort out

1. First I heard loud *lesly of gare.*
2. Then one of the men *riced out in nipa.*
3. After a few minutes his *smeracs* became fainter.

## 4. *Aussagen machen* – Making statements

| | |
|---|---|
| *eine Erklärung abgeben zu* | Mister Stoffel has made a statement on the outcome of the elections. |
| *etwas zugeben* | Stoffel admitted that he was responsible for the catastrophe. |
| *überzeugen von* | He had been unable to convince the voters of his programme. |
| *im Einzelnen besprechen / diskutieren* | Next week a party committee would discuss the outcome of the elections in more detail. |
| *ankündigen* | He was going to announce his retirement from politics. |
| *nach langer Diskussion über* | But after a long discussion on the future of the party ... |
| *überreden; überzeugen* | ... the party leader, Dr Kraut had persuaded him to stay on. |
| *zusichern; versichern* | He assured Dr Kraut of his loyalty and cooperation. |
| *betonen* | Stoffel stressed the importance of discipline and courage. |
| *Tatsachen feststellen* | He added that he hadn't intended to hurt his opponent's feelings, he had only stated facts. |
| *etwas dagegen haben; einwenden* | He personally didn't object to being attacked by political opponents. |
| *sich beklagen über* | In politics one shouldn't complain about harsh criticism. |

### Time for a smile

He went to the newspaper office to put an ad in the paper offering $5.0000 reward for the return of his wife's cat. The man behind the counter said: "That's a lot of reward isn't it?" He said: "It doesn't matter. I drowned the cat."

13

## LEVEL (m)

At the Italian restaurant, Bob and Ron:

**R:** My goodness, Bob, this place *is as silent as the grave.* There's nobody around.

**B:** That's right. Since the terror attacks people don't go out any more.

**R:** And people *have got wind* of the fact that the terrorists are sending out anthrax germs by mail.

**B:** Well, these things are destroying business. *Between you, me and the bedpost,* I think we'll go into a very deep recession.

### 1. Silence is golden – *Schweigen ist Gold*

| | |
|---|---|
| silence is golden | *Reden ist Silber, Schweigen ist Gold* |
| hear a pin drop | *eine Stecknadel fallen hören* |
| a pregnant pause / silence | *eine nachdenkliche Stille* |
| be as silent as the grave | *totenstill sein* |
| hold one's peace | *für immer schweigen* |
| pipe down | *still sein; die Klappe halten* |
| keep one's own counsel | *seine Meinung für sich behalten* |
| Mum's the word! | *Nichts verraten!* |
| not breathe a word of / about something | *kein Sterbenswörtchen über etwas sagen* |
| keep something under one's hat | *etwas für sich behalten* |
| keep one's trap / mouth shut | *den Mund halten* |
| hold one's tongue | *seinen Mund halten* |
| rather swallow one's tongue than say anything | *sich eher die Zunge abbeißen als etwas sagen* |
| button one's lips / mouth | *seine Lippen versiegeln* |
| His lips are sealed. | *Er ist verschwiegen wie ein Grab.* |
| take one's secret into the grave | *ein Geheimnis mit ins Grab nehmen* |
| keep something under wraps | *etwas geheim halten / für sich behalten* |
| keep the lid on something | *etwas unter Verschluss halten* |
| Actions speak louder than words. | *Taten zählen mehr als Worte. Es gibt nichts Gutes, außer man tut es.* |

## QUICK CHECK 6: Silly questions

1. What is golden? ....................
2. What can you sometimes hear drop? ....................
3. Where do some people take their secrets? ....................
4. What speak louder than words? ....................

## QUICK CHECK 7: What's the *woggle*?

Bob and Ron discuss Ron's business problems:

**B:** Didn't you get an appointment with the Chairman of the Board?
**R:** Next week. But at present my customer *is woggling its own counsel.* They're saying nothing.
**B:** I think they're trying to *keep the woggle on* their own bad management.
**R:** You're probably right. But that doesn't help. I need to know things. In this situation *silence* certainly *is not wogglen.*

### TIME FOR A SMILE

*My friend Harvey*

He thinks that electricity was invented by Voltaire.
He thinks that Robinson Crusoe was a world-famous tenor.
He thinks Karl Marx was the brother of Chico and Harpo.

## 2. Hearing and listening – *Hören und zuhören*

| | |
|---|---|
| have one's ear to the ground | *die Ohren offen halten* |
| see through a brick wall | *das Gras wachsen hören* |
| hang on someone's (every) word | *an jemandes Lippen hängen* |
| prick up one's ears | *die Ohren spitzen; aufhorchen* |
| lend an ear to someone | *jemandem zuhören* |
| get someone's ear | *jemandes Aufmerksamkeit erregen* |
| catch / notice what someone says | *aufschnappen, was jemand sagt* |
| get wind of | *Wind bekommen von* |
| hear by word of mouth | *vom Hörensagen wissen* |
| be as deaf as a doorpost | *taub wie eine Nuss sein; stocktaub sein* |

13

| | |
|---|---|
| get the wrong end of the stick | *etwas in den falschen Hals kriegen* |
| talk to the winds | *tauben Ohren predigen* |
| fall on deaf ears | *kein Gehör finden* |
| turn a deaf ear | *sich taub stellen* |
| It's like talking to a brick wall. | *Es ist, als würde man gegen eine Wand reden.* |
| In one ear, out of the other. | *Zum einen Ohr hinein, zum andern hinaus.* |
| drown someone out | *jemanden übertönen* |

## QUICK CHECK 8: What can you do with brick walls?

1. You can .................... your head against a brick wall trying to achieve something impossible.
2. Sometimes people, especially teachers have to .................... to a brick wall.
3. Some journalists think they can .................... through a brick wall.

## QUICK CHECK 9: Remember the idioms?

Boyfriend problems, Bob and Ron.

**B:** So Steffi's got a new boyfriend. It's terrible. She (*an seinen Lippen hängen*).

**R:** You mean she doesn't listen to you any more, which is probably better anyway since you always (*alles in den falschen Hals kriegen*).

**B:** That's not true. Anyway, I've tried to warn her about some things, but (*zu einem Ohr rein-, zum anderen rausgehen*). She doesn't listen.

## 3. Losing and finding one's voice – *Seine Sprache verlieren und wiederfinden*

| | |
|---|---|
| be tongue-tied | *keinen Ton herausbringen* |
| (not) get a word in edgewise / edgeways | *nicht zu Worte kommen* |
| have a frog in one's throat | *einen Frosch im Hals haben* |
| clear one's throat | *sich räuspern; sich bemerkbar machen* |
| find one's voice / tongue | *seine Sprache wiederfinden* |
| break the silence | *das Schweigen brechen* |
| break the ice | *die anfängliche Zurückhaltung überwinden; das Eis brechen* |
| roll / slip / trip off the tongue | *leicht über die Lippen kommen* |
| have the gift of the gab | *redegewandt sein* |
| sight-read | *vom Blatt "singen"* |
| chip in | *sich mit seiner Meinung einmischen* |
| speak off the cuff | *aus dem Handgelenk / Stegreif reden* |
| lower one's voice | *die Stimme senken; leiser reden* |
| talk the hind legs off a donkey | *jemandem ein Loch in den Bauch reden* |
| spill the beans | *alles ausplaudern; sich verplappern* |
| shout at the top of one's voice | *aus vollem Halse brüllen / schreien* |

### DOUBLE CHECK 10: Nerves

I've got to make a presentation next week, but I'm really nervous about it. I'm completely ....................*-tied* at the moment. And I don't like *speaking off the* .................... to large groups. I'm better at speaking to individuals privately. That's no problem, but with fifty people in front of you, how do you start? And how do you .................... *the ice*?

## 4. In strict confidence – *Ganz im Vertrauen*

| | |
|---|---|
| I'd like a word with you. | *Ich habe mit dir zu reden.* |
| have a word in someone's ear | *jemandem etwas im Vertrauen / unter vier Augen sagen* |
| get it (things) off one's chest | *sich etwas von der Seele reden; etwas loswerden* |
| between you, me and the bedpost / doorpost | *unter uns / im Vertrauen gesagt* |
| talk behind closed doors | *hinter verschlossenen Türen etwas besprechen* |
| speak to someone in private | *sich mit jemandem vertraulich unterhalten* |
| play one's cards close to one's chest | *mit verdeckten Karten spielen* |
| chew the fat / rag | *quatschen; plaudern; nörgeln* |
| talk behind someone's back | *über jemanden hinter seinem Rücken reden* |

### DOUBLE CHECK 11: Parts of the body

Paula and Jean on mobbing.

**P:** Jean, *can I have a word in your* ............................?

**J:** Sure. You look stressed. Have you got something you *want to get off your* ............................?

**P:** Yes I have. It's Tom, our new manager. He's mobbing me. He started it when I refused to go out with him.

**J:** Well, that probably explains it. You know he's always *talking about you behind your* ............................ .

**P:** You're joking. I didn't know that.

### Time for a smile

My lawyer's beyond brilliant. In a recent case some of you may have read about, he told his client, "Don't worry. The judge is my cousin. Their chief witness goes with my secretary. And I'm planning to bribe four of the jurors. Meanwhile, try to escape!"

## 5. Ways of saying it – *Der Ton macht die Musik*

| | |
|---|---|
| talk over everybody's head | *über die Köpfe hinwegreden* |
| spin a yarn | *eine Geschichte erzählen; Seemannsgarn spinnen* |
| That's the long and the short of it. | *Das ist die ganze Geschichte; mit einem Wort; kurzum* |
| talk shop | *übers Geschäft reden; fachsimpeln* |
| talk off the top of one's head | *aus dem hohlen Bauch reden* |
| have a sharp tongue | *eine scharfe Zunge haben* |
| beat about / around the bush | *um den heißen Brei herumreden* |
| call a spade a spade | *das Kind beim Namen nennen* |
| say something under one's breath | *hinter vorgehaltener Hand sagen* |
| name names | *Namen nennen; aus dem Nähkästchen plaudern* |
| speak all in one breath | *in einem Atemzug sagen* |
| ramble on | *drauflosreden; ohne Punkt und Komma reden* |
| rattle something off | *(eine Rede) herunterrasseln* |
| speak out of turn | *unpassende Bemerkungen machen* |
| blow one's own horn / trumpet | *ins eigene Horn stoßen; sich selbst loben* |
| talking rubbish | *Blech reden* |
| waste one's breath | *in den Wind reden* |
| shoot off one's mouth | *das Maul aufreißen; den Mund voll nehmen* |
| say with (one's) tongue in (one's) cheek | *ironisch sagen* |
| keep a civil tongue in one's head | *höflich bleiben* |
| speak volumes | *Bände sprechen* |
| be a slip of the tongue | *ein Versprecher sein* |
| bite one's tongue | *sich auf die Zunge beißen* |
| yell / scream one's head off | *sich die Lunge aus dem Leib schreien* |
| cut somebody short | *jemandem in die Rede fallen; das Wort abschneiden* |
| put in a good word for someone | *für jemanden ein gutes Wort einlegen* |
| Mind / watch your tongue! | *Hüte deine Zunge!; Überlege dir, was du sagst.* |
| Mind your language! | *Drück dich gefälligst anständig aus!* |

## DOUBLE CHECK 12: Silly questions

1. What do too many politicians blow? ......................................
2. What should politicians always call a spade? ......................................
3. What do most politicians beat about or around when asked any questions? ......................................

**TIME FOR A SMILE**

You should be a little suspicious of your wife if she asks for her weekly household money in traveller's checks.

## 6. Letting them know – *Informieren*

| | |
|---|---|
| spill the beans | *etwas ausplaudern* |
| give someone the run-down on something | *jemanden ins Bild setzen über etwas* |
| update someone | *jemanden auf den neuesten Stand bringen* |
| give someone the low-down on something | *jemandem die Hintergrundinformationen über etwas geben* |
| fill someone in on something | *jemanden über etwas unterrichten* |
| put someone in the picture on / about | *jemanden in Kenntnis setzen über* |
| keep someone posted about something | *jemanden über etwas auf dem Laufenden halten* |
| clue someone up (sl) | *jemanden ins Bild setzen* |
| get something straight from the horse's mouth | *etwas aus erster Quelle erfahren* |
| put two and two together | *eins und eins zusammenzählen* |
| drive / bring something home | *etwas nachdrücklich vor Augen führen* |
| zoom in on | *sich näher befassen mit; näher eingehen auf* |
| have a heart-to-heart | *ein offenes Gespräch führen* |
| touch on something | *etwas nur kurz erwähnen / ansprechen* |
| come clean (with the facts) | *auspacken; mit der Wahrheit rausrücken* |

| | |
|---|---|
| break the news to someone | *jemandem die schlechte Nachricht beibringen* |
| News certainly travels fast! | *Neuigkeiten verbreiten sich wie ein Lauffeuer!* |
| let the cat out of the bag | *die Katze aus dem Sack lassen* |
| blow the gaff | *ein Geheimnis ausplaudern* |
| the latest gossip | *der neueste Klatsch* |
| hear it on the grapevine | *etwas gerüchteweise hören* |

## DOUBLE CHECK 13: Scrambled idioms

Clear up the mess. Words have gone into the wrong places.

Love hurts – Anne and Bob:

**A:** Did you hear *the latest grapevine*?
**B:** No, but I'm sure you'll *keep me broke.*
**A:** Yes. Bryan and Liz are splitting up. They are getting a divorce.
**B:** You're not certain. You probably *heard it on the gossip* somewhere.
**A:** That's not true. Liz *posted the news to me* yesterday on the phone.
**B:** I was wondering about them. They're always arguing.

## 7. Avoiding the truth – *Der Wahrheit aus dem Weg gehen*

| | |
|---|---|
| lie / bluff one's way out of something | *sich aus einer Sache herauslügen* |
| Once a liar, always a liar. | *Wer einmal lügt, dem glaubt man nicht.* |
| tell someone a pack of lies | *jemandem die Hucke voll lügen* |
| give the lie to something | *eine Sache Lügen strafen* |
| lie through one's teeth | *lügen wie gedruckt; das Blaue vom Himmel lügen* |
| take someone for a ride | *jemanden auf den Arm nehmen; jemanden betrügen* |
| welsh on someone | *sein Wort nicht halten; jemanden sitzen lassen* |
| lead someone up / down the garden path | *jemanden hinters Licht führen / an der Nase herumführen* |

13

| | |
|---|---|
| tell a white lie | *eine Notlüge gebrauchen* |
| feed someone a line | *jemandem einen Bären aufbinden* |
| bend the truth | *sehr locker mit der Wahrheit umgehen* |
| Tell that to the marines! | *Das kannst du deiner Großmutter erzählen!* |

## DOUBLE CHECK 14: Let's go *woggling* again

The English teacher. Ortrud and Ron:

**O:** That Englishman certainly *took us for a woggle.* He cost us a lot of money, too.

**R:** Well, *he fed me a woggle* about his whole qualifications.

**O:** And with the airplane ticket, too.

**R:** He *was lying through his woggles* when he accepted the job. Sometimes I can't understand people.

### Time for a smile

Time may be a great healer, but it's a lousy beautician.

## 8. Gossips and gasbags – *Klatschbasen und Quasseltanten*

| | |
|---|---|
| talk a lot of hot air | *dumm daherschwätzen* |
| talk nineteen to a dozen | *wie ein Wasserfall reden* |
| rabbit on (about something) | *fortdauernd quatschen* |
| talk one's head off | *jemandem Löcher in den Bauch reden; reden wie ein Wasserfall* |
| talk through one's hat; talk through one's arse (sl) | *dummes Zeug / Schwachsinn reden* |
| That'll have plenty of tongues wagging. | *Darüber werden sich viele die Mäuler zerreißen.* |
| bend someone's ear | *pausenlos auf jemanden einreden* |
| chew someone's ears off | *jemandem die Ohren voll jammern und sich beschweren* |

| | |
|---|---|
| swear like a trooper / fishwife | *wie ein Rohrspatz schimpfen* |
| spread gossip | *alles weitertratschen* |
| be a chatterbox | *ein Plappermaul / eine Quasselstrippe sein* |
| be all talk and no action | *viel Reden, aber nichts tun* |

## DOUBLE CHECK 15: Your choice again

Loud mouths. Bob and Ron at the sauna:

**B:** I'm glad Pete has left. *He talked a lot of hot*
**A.** *air* **B.** *gas* **C.** *smoke.*

**R:** You're right. He *was* always
**A.** *parrotting on* **B.** *rabbiting on* **C.** *ratting on* about something or other.

**B:** And what I couldn't stand was the bad language. He *swears like a*
**A.** *taxi driver* **B.** *soldier* **C.** *trooper.*

**R:** Yes, that certainly is frustrating. But he's left the club now anyway.

# Around our money

## *Rund um unser Geld*

14

BIRD'S EYE VIEW

### LEVEL 1

1. *Kleider kaufen* – Buying clothes
2. *Dies und das kaufen* – Buying this and that
3. *An der Kasse* – At the check-out

### LEVEL 2

1. The way we dress – *Wie wir uns kleiden*
2. Striking a good bargain – *Ein Schnäppchen machen*
3. A bad buy – *Ein schlechter Kauf*
4. Selling – *Verkaufen*

### TIME FOR A SMILE

***Murphy's Law about buying clothes***

If you like it, they don't have it in your size.
If you like it and it's in your size, it doesn't fit anyway.
If you like it and it fits, you can't afford it.
If it fits, it's ugly.
If you like it, it fits and you can afford it, it falls apart the first time you wear it.

**LEVEL** **14**

If you have money you probably want to go shopping to try to find this bargain or that one. You can sometimes get something good for your money in large stores but you have to be careful. Don't put your items into your basket before you pass through the check-out. And remember in England you can always pay by credit-card. You don't need to pay cash.

## 1. *Kleider kaufen* – Buying clothes

| | |
|---|---|
| *einkaufen gehen* | I feel like going shopping. |
| *sich gut kleiden* | Tina's always very elegant. She dresses so well. |
| *einen teuren Geschmack haben* | She spends Tom's salary on dresses. She has expensive tastes. |
| *eine Größe tragen* | What size do you take? – I take a size 52. |
| *zu weit an den Schultern* | I'm afraid the shirt is too wide across the shoulders. |
| *Größe 48.* | Try a size 54. |
| *drücken; zu eng sein* | These shoes are too narrow. They pinch. |
| *eine Nummer größer* | I'm afraid these shoes are too small. I need the next size. |
| *umtauschen* | I'd like to change these trousers. They are not my size. I need the next size. |
| *Der Anzug sitzt nicht gut.* | I'm afraid the suit doesn't fit me very well. |
| *etwas Billigeres* | Haven't you got anything cheaper? |
| *gut passen zu* | This blouse goes nicely with your skirt. |
| *ändern lassen* | Could I have the jacket altered? |
| *für Änderungen bezahlen* | Do I have to pay for alterations? |
| *ändern ohne Aufpreis* | The skirt can be altered at no extra charge. |
| *Gibt es diese Strickjacke in anderen Farben?* | Is this cardigan available in other colours? |
| *Wie wäre es mit Gelb?* | What about something in yellow? |
| *ein Schnäppchen* | Look at this raincoat. It's a real bargain. |
| *ins Hotel schicken* | Could you send these things to the hotel, please? |

## QUICK CHECK 1: Pitfalls for Germans

Is it A or B?

1. These shoes pinch. I'm afraid these shoes are too **A.** *small* **B.** *little.*
2. Could you **A.** *alter* **B.** *change* these trousers? I need the next size.
3. Tina's always very elegant. She dresses so **A.** *good* **B.** *well.*

TIME FOR A SMILE

***Good bargains***

A bargain is something you buy that is cheaper than something you really want or need.

## 2. *Dies und das kaufen* – Buying this and that

| | |
|---|---|
| *an der Reihe sein* | I think it's my turn. |
| *Wie viel kostet das?* | I'll take the camera and a film. How much is that altogether? |
| *etwas brauchen* | I need a street map of London. |
| *einen Film entwickeln* | Could you develop this film, please? |
| *Wie lange dauert es?* | How long will it take? |
| *Abzug vom Negativ* | Could you develop this film? One print of every negative. |
| *Könnte ich eine Plastiktüte haben?* | Could you give me a plastic bag, please? |
| *als Geschenk einpacken* | Could you gift-wrap it, please? |
| *schicken lassen?* | Could I have these books sent to this address? |
| *etwas auf Lager haben* | Do you have any A4 paper in stock? |
| *noch etwas übrig haben* | I wonder if you have any of that good cheddar cheese left? |

## QUICK CHECK 2: What to say in these situations

| The problem | What to say |
|---|---|
| Your raincoat is dirty. | I'd like to .................. my raincoat .................. . |
| The skirt doesn't fit, but you want it after all. | Could you .................. this skirt? |
| The article is a bit too expensive. | Haven't you ..................? |
| You want to send it as a present. | Can you ........................? |
| It's too heavy and your hotel is far away. | Could I ................ this ................ my hotel? |

## 3. *An der Kasse* – At the check-out

| | |
|---|---|
| *Zahlungsbedingungen* | What are your terms / conditions of payment? |
| *Skonto gewähren* | Do you allow / grant / give a prompt payment discount? |
| *Skonto bei Barzahlung* | Do you offer a cash discount? |
| *Mengenrabatt geben* | Is there a quantity / bulk discount for ...? |
| *zu viel kosten* | So you think it costs too much. |
| *Der Preis hängt von der Größe Ihres Auftrags ab.* | The price depends on the size of order you want to place. |
| *eine Anzahlung verlangen* | We require a deposit of 10 percent. |
| *den Rest nach Lieferung bezahlen* | You can pay the rest after delivery. |
| *im Voraus bar bezahlen* | You must pay cash up front if you want to take it away. |
| *bar zahlen* | I never pay cash. I always pay by cheque or by credit card. |
| *im Voraus bezahlen* | Do you want me to pay in advance? |
| *Wie viel macht das alles zusammen?* | How much is that altogether? |
| *kanadische Dollars nehmen* | Do you accept / take Canadian dollars? |
| *mit Kreditkarte zahlen* | I'd like to pay by credit card. |

| | |
|---|---|
| *sein Geld wert sein* | You'll find out that you get good value for money from this product. |
| *das Geld bar auf den Tisch des Hauses blättern* | pay cash on the nail |
| *etwas auf Pump kaufen* | buy / get something on tick |
| *auf Raten / kleckerweise kaufen* | buy (pay) in dribs and drabs |
| *auf Raten kaufen* | buy on HP (hire purchase) / the drip |

## QUICK CHECK 3: Beef up your word power

Find a phrase that has the same meaning:

| | |
|---|---|
| Can I help you? | What *can I* ..................*?* |
| I think I was next. | I think it's .................. . |
| We need a deposit of 10%. | We ............... a deposit of 10%. |
| When will it be ready? | How long .................. ? |

## QUICK CHECK 4: One word for four idioms

1. How long will it .....................................?
2. What size do you .....................................?
3. I'll ..................................... this cardigan.
4. Do you ..................................... Swiss Franks?

### Time for a smile

***VIPs on food***

I just love Chinese food. My favourite dish is 27.
*Clement Atlee*

I will not eat oysters. I want my food dead. Not sick, not wounded, dead. *Woody Allen*

McDonald's in Tokyo is a terrible revenge for Pearl Harbor.
*S. I. Hayakawa*

**LEVEL**

It's especially difficult to be sure you're not *paying through the nose* when you buy second-hand goods. Someone may be *taking you for a ride.* And when you've paid your money you're often *stuck with the goods.* Be very careful with used cars. Some salesmen are almost corrupt. They would *sell their own grandmothers.* It's almost unbelievable what junk they try to *fob off* on naïve but innocent people.

## 1. The way we dress – *Wie wir uns kleiden*

| | |
|---|---|
| be in fashion | *mit der Mode gehen* |
| be dressed to the nines | *aufgedonnert sein* |
| be dressed to kill | *todschick gekleidet sein; aufgeputzt sein* |
| put on one's Sunday best | *den Sonntagsstaat anlegen* |
| tog oneself out / up | *sich in Schale werfen* |
| be spruced up | *geschniegelt und gebügelt sein* |
| not a hair out of place | *wie aus dem Ei gepellt* |
| Fine feathers make fine birds. | *Kleider machen Leute.* |
| suit someone down to the ground | *genau das Richtige für jemanden sein* |
| be tailor-made | *maßgeschneidert sein* |
| fit someone like a glove | *jemandem wie angegossen passen* |
| be in one's birthday suit | *im Adams- / Evakostüm dastehen* |
| wear hand-me-downs | *abgelegte Kleider tragen* |
| look a sight | *einen schrecklichen Anblick bieten; schrecklich aussehen* |
| look the worse for wear | *heruntergekommen / mitgenommen aussehen* |
| look like one was dragged through the hedge backwards | *völlig zerrupft und zerfleddert aussehen* |
| be down at heel | *heruntergekommen sein* |

## QUICK CHECK 5: Remember the idiom?

Jake and Lyn have just met Rob:

J: My God. I'd never have expected it. Rob seems to be really *down at* ...................................... .

L: I think he's wearing ..................*-me-*.................. .

J: Something's happened. He was never short of a bob or two. And all his clothes were *tailor-*...................................... .

L: I bet he's gone bankrupt.

## QUICK CHECK 6: Silly questions

1. How should a suit fit you? ......................................
2. What do fine feathers make? ......................................
3. He looks as if he was dragged through what? ...............................

## 2. Striking a good bargain – *Ein Schnäppchen machen*

| | |
|---|---|
| First come, first served. | *Wer zuerst kommt, mahlt zuerst.* |
| Don't look a gift horse in the mouth. | *Einem geschenkten Gaul schaut man nicht ins Maul.* |
| get it for next to nothing | *etwas fast umsonst bekommen* |
| It's going for a song. | *Das bekommt man für ein Butterbrot.* |
| at a throwaway price | *zum Schleuderpreis* |
| get one's money's worth | *etwas für sein Geld bekommen* |
| get value for money | *reell / preiswert bedient werden* |
| offer a knock-down / giveaway / throwaway price | *Einführungs- / Schleuderpreis anbieten* |
| jump at an offer | *bei einem Angebot schnell zugreifen* |
| offer the chance of a lifetime | *eine einmalige Chance bieten* |
| cut prices | *mit den Preisen runtergehen* |
| It's a snip / bargain. | *Das ist ein Schnäppchen.* |
| come halfway on the price | *beim Preis auf halbem Wege entgegenkommen* |
| It suits me to a T. | *Das ist haargenau das Richtige.* |

## QUICK CHECK 7: What's the *woggle*?

Bob and Anne shopping:

**A:** Look at this lovely dress. And *it's going for* a *woggle.*

**B:** What do you want to buy clothes for? You won't fit them next week the way you're losing weight. And it's typical of you to *woggle at every offer* you see.

**A:** That's not fair! It's a *woggle price*. And you're only jealous about my weight.

**B:** Okay, okay. I must admit the dress *suits you to a woggle.*

## 3. A bad buy – *Ein schlechter Kauf*

| | |
|---|---|
| buy a shelf-warmer | *einen Ladenhüter kaufen* |
| buy a pig in a poke | *die Katze im Sack kaufen* |
| fall for it | *darauf hereinfallen* |
| That's a fake / forgery | *Das ist ja eine Fälschung.* |
| buy a white elephant | *ein Groschengrab / einen lästigen, kostspieligen Besitz erwerben* |
| buy trash / rubbish / junk | *Schund kaufen* |
| cost an arm and a leg | *ein Vermögen kosten* |
| cost a pretty penny | *ein schönes Stück Geld kosten* |
| cost a packet | *eine Stange Geld kosten* |
| be a smack in the face | *ein Schlag ins Gesicht sein* |
| Prices go through the roof. | *Preise steigen Schwindel erregend.* |
| pay through the nose | *bluten / blechen müssen* |
| dip into one's pocket | *(tief) in die eigene Tasche greifen* |
| hike / jack up the prices | *Preise erhöhen* |
| It's a bit steep. | *Das ist ganz schön happig / gesalzen.* |
| That's a rip-off. | *Das ist Wucher.* |
| The price is over the top. | *Der Preis ist unverschämt.* |

## QUICK CHECK 8: Animal idioms

1. I'd see the car first. I'm not going to buy a .................. in a .................. .
2. I can't afford a Rolls Royce. It's a .................. .
3. Don't look a .................. in the mouth.
4. Fine .................. make fine .................. .

## QUICK CHECK 9: Correct the mistakes

Ron talks about selling copiers:

The market's broken down. And the euro's so strong. It means our copiers *cost a leg and an arm* in the US. And now our sales department has *hacked up the prizes* again. No wonder we can't sell anything. And then the terrorist attacks. That's the next *box in the face.* Nobody wants to travel.

TIME FOR A SMILE

Selling is the most exciting thing
you can do with your clothes on.
*John Fenton*

## 4. Selling – *Verkaufen*

| | |
|---|---|
| sell one's own grandmother | *seine eigene Großmutter verkaufen* |
| two for the price of one | *zwei zum Preis von einem* |
| sell at a dumping price | *unter Selbstkosten / zu Schleuderpreisen verkaufen* |
| land an order | *einen Auftrag ergattern / an Land ziehen* |
| change hands | *den Besitzer wechseln* |
| meet someone's needs | *jemandes Bedürfnisse befriedigen* |
| meet / cover the demand | *den Bedarf decken* |
| push / boost sales | *den Verkauf ankurbeln* |
| scrape the bottom of the barrel | *den letzten schäbigen Rest zusammenkratzen* |
| be a tough salesman | *ein abgebrühter Verkäufer sein* |
| pull the wool over someone's eyes | *jemanden hinters Licht führen* |
| rip someone off | *jemanden übers Ohr hauen / neppen* |

| | |
|---|---|
| sell under the counter | *unter der Hand / dem Ladentisch verkaufen* |
| throw dust in someone's eyes | *jemandem Sand in die Augen streuen* |
| talk someone into buying something | *jemandem etwas aufschwatzen* |
| railroad someone into buying something | *jemandem etwas aufdrängen* |
| fob something off on someone | *jemandem etwas andrehen* |
| fleece someone | *jemanden ausnehmen* |
| sell someone short | *jemanden übers Ohr hauen* |
| to take someone for a ride | *jemanden reinlegen* |
| sell someone a pup | *jemandem Ramsch andrehen* |
| be as common as muck (sl) | *Dutzendware sein* |
| get stuck with the goods | *auf der Ware sitzen bleiben* |
| get / gain the edge over one's competitors | *die Konkurrenz überflügeln* |
| fetch a good price | *einen guten Preis erzielen* |
| be a good seller | *sich gut verkaufen* |
| be a money spinner | *ein Renner sein* |
| be a cash-cow | *ein Goldesel sein* |
| sell like hot cakes | *weggehen wie warme Semmeln* |
| Sales are rocketing. | *Der Absatz schnellt in die Höhe.* |
| Don't count your chickens before they're hatched. | *Verkaufe das Fell nicht, bevor du den Bären erlegt hast.* |

## TIME FOR A SMILE

***A good bargain***

The following conversation took place at a Rolls Royce car showroom: "If I buy one of these cars on credit," asked a customer, "how long will I have to pay for it?"
"It depends on how much you can pay each month," replied the salesman.
The man paused, "25 pounds, more or less."
"Well then," said the salesman laughing, "it will take you about a hundred years."
"Excellent. Let's sign the contract."

## QUICK CHECK 10: Take a vowel for an x

Dangerous business, Tim and Annette:

**T:** So you've bought that car. I think you've been *sxld a pxp.*

**A:** What do you mean? The salesman told me he'd *sxld it at a lxss.*

**T:** I bet he did. But look at it. He's *pxllxd the wxxl xvxr your xyxs*! Look at the milometer. Twenty thousand. That's simply not possible!

## QUICK CHECK 11: Tim, the 'yes-man'

Complete Tim's idiomatic echo.

**1.**

**Tom:** Tina wants to buy that penthouse from the White Elephant Agency. I'm afraid the prices of property have *risen very rapidly.*

**Tim:** Yes, I know. Property prices have gone *through the* ....................... .

**2.**

**Tom:** She thinks that penthouse is an *exceptional opportunity.*

**Tim:** Yes, she thinks it's the ....................... of a ....................... .

**3.**

**Tom:** She'll pay *far too much money* for a house in that neighbourhood.

**Tim:** She'll pay ....................... *the* ....................... for a house in that area.

**4.**

**Tom:** And the repairs alone will *cost a large sum of money.*

**Tim:** The repairs will cost an ....................... and a ....................... .

**5.**

**Tom:** I suppose her fiancé *forced her to* buy it.

**Tim:** Sure. Her fiancé must have ....................... her into buying it.

**6.**

**Tom:** Poor Tina! The White Elephant Agency will sell her *a house that is worth much less than the price she'll pay for the repairs.*

**Tim:** Yes, they will sell her *a* ....................... .

# The World of work

## *Die Welt der Arbeit*

15

### Bird's eye view

#### LEVEL 1

1. *Arbeitsplatz und Arbeitszeit* – Working place and working hours
2. *Berufe* – Jobs and professions
3. *Ausbildung* – Training
4. *Die Stelle bekommen* – Getting the job
5. *Das Auf und Ab* – The ups and downs
6. *Verhältnis Arbeitgeber – Arbeitnehmer* – Industrial relations
7. *Sich selbständig machen* – Becoming self-employed

#### LEVEL 2

1. Years of apprenticeship – *Lehrjahre*
2. Filling a vacancy – *Eine Stelle besetzen*
3. Good workers – *Gute Arbeiter*
4. Bad workers – *Schlechte Arbeiter*
5. Firing – *Entlassen*

### Time for a smile

The director of a toilet-paper factory was giving a review of business: "Consumption of our brand of toilet-paper in the past year amounted to 1.5 kilos per head." One of the workers asked, "I don't understand. Why per head?"

## LEVEL 1

The interviewee, Ivan; Interviewer, Tom:

**I:** So, until now you've only done part-time work. Is that right?
**T:** Well, I've also done quite a lot of manual work to make a living.
**I:** That doesn't help much, I'm afraid. Different type of work. I notice you've changed jobs quite a lot. Why was that?
**T:** Oh, that was because I was always too qualified for the job.

### 1. *Arbeitsplatz und Arbeitszeit* – Working place and working hours

| | |
|---|---|
| *Kaufhaus* | Tina works in the office of a big department store. |
| *eine Halbtagsstelle haben* | Tina works part-time because Tom's wages aren't high enough. |
| *gleitende Arbeitszeit haben* | And Tina can work flexitime. |
| *ganztags arbeiten* | Tom works full-time. His wife Tina only works part-time. |
| *Überstunden machen* | Tom didn't want to work / do overtime. So he gave in his notice. |
| *Schicht arbeiten* | At the moment, Tom is doing shifts in a coal mine. |
| *Nachtschicht* | Tom hates the night shifts. |
| *unbezahlte Überstunden machen* | He does a lot of unpaid overtime. |
| *hinter verschlossenen Türen arbeiten* | He works behind closed doors. |
| *mit Stechuhr arbeiten* | Regular workers must clock in and clock out. |
| *Arbeitsbedingungen* | We've got lousy working conditions. |

**TIME FOR A SMILE**

Did you hear about the policeman who gave out a hundred parking tickets before he realised he was at a drive-in movie?

## QUICK CHECK 1: Hard times



1. working the whole of the day and week:
   Tom works ............................................ .
2. starting and finishing work at different times, but working a certain number of hours in a week or month:
   Tina can work ............................................ .
3. working for only a part of the day or week:
   Anne can work .................................... .
4. time worked in addition to one's normal working hours:
   John wanted to .................................... ...... . He needed the money.

### TIME FOR A SMILE

The first 90 percent of the task takes 90 percent of the time, the last 10 percent takes the other 90 percent. *A. Bloch*

## 2. *Berufe* – Jobs and professions

| | |
|---|---|
| *Was für einen Beruf haben Sie?* | What sort of job have you got? – I've a fascinating job. |
| *Was sind Sie von Beruf?* | What is your job? – I'm a clerk. I work in a bank. |
| *seinen Lebensunterhalt verdienen* | Tina's father wanted to know what Tom did for a living. |
| *akademischer Beruf* | Tina's father is a teacher by profession. |
| *handwerklicher Beruf* | Tom's father is a gardener by trade. |
| *Handwerker alter Schule* | Tom's father is a craftsman of the old school. |
| *Büroangestellter* | White collar workers have a desk job. |
| *Arbeiter* | Blue collar workers work on the shop floor. |
| *Wasserrohre verlegen* | A plumber repairs and fits water pipes. |
| *die Beleuchtung reparieren* | An electrician repairs the electric lighting. |
| *einen Rechtsanwalt konsultieren* | Consult a lawyer when you have problems with the police. |
| *Beamter auf Lebenszeit* | Tom's father is a civil servant for life. |
| *Ich war berufen für diese Arbeit.* | I had a calling to this job. |

## QUICK CHECK 2: The little difference

1. A bank clerk is a .............. .............. *worker.* He has a desk job.
2. A mechanic is a .............. .............. *worker.* He works on the shop-floor.
3. A police officer is a .............. .............. . He is employed by the government.

TIME FOR A SMILE

***The figure π and the researchers***

Mathematician: π is the number expressing the relationship between the circumference of a circle and its diameter.
Physicist: π is 3.1415927 plus or minus 0.000000005.
Engineer: π is about 3.

## 3. *Ausbildung* – Training

| | |
|---|---|
| *sich für ein Stipendium bewerben* | I've applied for a scholarship. I need the money badly. |
| *Stipendium erhalten* | Will Tim get a scholarship? – Maybe, he's applied for one. |
| *immatrikuliert sein* | How many students are enrolled at this university? |
| *mit einem Diplom abschließen* | After four years he took a degree in biology. |
| *Fertigkeit* | Typing is a basic skill in many jobs. |
| *Berufslaufbahn* | What sort of career would you choose? – I want to be a journalist. |
| *einen Beruf erlernen* | What are you training for? – I'm training to be a mechanic. |
| *einen Beruf erlernen* | What trade have you trained for? – I've trained to be a cook. |
| *Lehrling werden* | Tom became an apprentice in a carpenter's shop. |
| *ein Banklehre machen* | My dad trained as a bank clerk. |
| *Meister* | A master is a skilled workman who may train apprentices. |

| | |
|---|---|
| *eine Lehre machen* | Tom was serving his apprenticeship as a carpenter. |
| *sich um eine Stelle bewerben* | After his apprenticeship, Tom applied for a job in a factory. |
| *eine Bewerbung verschicken* | Tom sent his application to five companies. |
| *von der Handelskammer geprüft werden* | He was tested by the Chamber of Commerce. |

## QUICK CHECK 3: First rungs of the career ladder

1. First you ................................ for a scholarship.
2. Then you ................................ at a university.
3. Next you ................................ your degree.
4. And you ................................ a career.
5. Finally, you ............................ your application to several companies.

**TIME FOR A SMILE**

"We mustn't drink that much again," says Jones to Smith. "Do you remember that last night you sold Tower Bridge?"
"Is that all?"
"No, I bought it."

## 4. *Die Stelle bekommen* – Getting the job

| | |
|---|---|
| *gute Berufsaussichten* | Tina hopes that Tom will get a job with good prospects. |
| *Vorstellungsgespräch haben* | Next week Tom is having his job interview. |
| *eine Stelle anbieten* | Tom was offered a job in a carpenter's shop. |
| *offene Stelle* | The company had a vacancy for a carpenter with experience. |
| *Berufserfahrung haben* | Tom had some experience as a carpenter. |
| *einstellen; anstellen* | Tom got the job. He was employed because he was experienced. |

| | |
|---|---|
| *geeignet; qualifiziert sein* | The staff manager thought that he was qualified for the job. |
| *befördert werden* | As a carpenter you have no chances of promotion. |
| *Werkstatt* | Now Tom makes fine furniture in the carpenter's workshop. |
| *als freier Mitarbeiter arbeiten* | For two years Tina worked freelance for a big factory. |
| *als Selbständiger arbeiten* | John worked on a self-employed basis. |
| *eine Stelle bekommen* | She landed the job with a little help from her friends. |

## QUICK CHECK 4: Tim, the 'yes-man'

**1.**

**Bob:** Did you know that FSAB has *an opening* for a chemist with experience.
**Tim:** Yes, they have a .................................. for a chemist with experience.

**2.**

**Bob:** I think Tom will *get the job* with a little help from his friends.
**Tim:** Yes, I'm sure his friends will help him to ................................ *this job.*

**3.**

**Bob:** FSAB offer good chances of *quick promotion.*
**Tim:** Yes, they offer *good* .................................. .

### TIME FOR A SMILE

From the For Sale column of a Scottish newspaper:
For sale – second-hand tombstone, going cheap.
Great value for anybody named McTavish.
Owner going abroad.

## 5. *Das Auf und Ab* – The ups and downs

| | |
|---|---|
| *die Stelle wechseln* | After two years Tom changed jobs. |
| *Lohn erhöhen* | Tom changed jobs because his boss didn't increase his wages. |
| *kündigen* | Tom didn't get a wage increase so he handed / gave in his notice. |
| *Bezahlung ist nicht alles.* | Pay isn't everything. |
| *Arbeitsplatzbedingungen* | Working conditions are important, too. |
| *eine feste Arbeitsstelle* | At the moment, Tom hasn't got a steady job. |
| *befördert werden* | Tina was promoted. She got promotion after only one year. |
| *auf einer niedrigen Gehaltsstufe sein* | But she complained that she was in the low income bracket. |
| *einen freien Tag haben* | Tina had a day off. She wanted to visit her mother. |
| *in Ruhestand gehen* | Tom's father retired at the age of 62. |
| *Gehalt und Lohn* | By the way, a teacher gets a salary. A carpenter gets wages. |
| *Gehaltserhöhung bekommen* | Civil servants will receive no pay rise this year. |

### QUICK CHECK 5: Odd man out (they are even wrong)

**1.** He went to his boss and asked
**A.** for a pay rise
**B.** for a wage increase
**C.** for a money increase

**2.** If the boss said 'no' he would
**A.** announce that he is going to leave the firm
**B.** receive his pension
**C.** give in his notice

**3.** So his boss promoted him to the next higher
**A.** tax level
**B.** wage bracket
**C.** income bracket

## QUICK CHECK 6: Find the third man

| . . . . . . . . . . . . . . . | |
|---|---|
| wages | salary |

## 6. *Verhältnis Arbeitgeber – Arbeitnehmer* – Industrial relations

| | |
|---|---|
| *Gewerkschaftsmitglied sein* | Tom is a member of a Trade Union. |
| *arbeitslos sein* | Tom has been out of work for three months now. |
| *Arbeitslosenquote* | The unemployment rate in Germany in 2006 is almost 8 percent. |
| *gekündigt werden* | Hundreds of miners are given notice. |
| *Wochenarbeitszeit erhöhen* | Employers in Germany want to increase the weekly hours of work. |
| *zum Streik aufrufen* | The union called the workers out on strike |
| *Streik ausrufen* | The trade union is calling for a strike. They want more money. |
| *bessere Arbeitsplatz-bedingungen fordern* | We request / demand better working conditions for women. |
| *ein wilder Streik* | Some of the workers went on a wild cat strike. |
| *einstellen und entlassen* | Some companies hire employees and fire them after a year. |
| *entlassen werden* | The director of Tina's department store was dismissed. |
| *sich selbständig machen* | After years of unemployment Tom is trying to set up on his own. |
| *Arbeit suchen* | Jim is looking for a job. He's ready to accept any job. |
| *Betriebsrat* | He got a job as the works council. |
| *Gewerkschaftsvertreter* | He's the trade union representative. |

## QUICK CHECK 7: Pitfalls for Germans

1. Tom is *member* of a Trade Union.
2. Jim is *looking after* a job. He's ready to accept any job.
3. Tom has been out of work *since three months* now.

## QUICK CHECK 8: Beef up your word power

Find a phrase that has the same meaning.

| | |
|---|---|
| be unemployed | be ...................................................... |
| be fired | be ...................................................... |
| demand better conditions | ............................ better conditions |

## 7. *Sich selbständig machen* – Becoming self-employed

| | |
|---|---|
| *ein Geschäft übernehmen* | Finally, Tom took over the carpenter's shop of a retired carpenter. |
| *selbständig sein* | Tom is self-employed. He owns the carpenter's shop. |
| *konkurrieren mit* | Tom was in competition with other carpenters in the town. |
| *Einkommen; Verdienst* | At first Tom's earnings were very modest. |
| *Gewinn machen* | The first six months Tom made almost no profit. |
| *einen Betrieb leiten* | Tom didn't know how to run a business. |
| *ein verantwortlicher Posten* | Today he runs a company with 20 employees. It's a responsible job. |
| *das eigene Geschäft; die eigene Firma* | You take a big risk when it's your own business. |
| *ins kalte Wasser springen* | He had to jump in at the deep end. |
| *sich voll einsetzen; seinen Mann stehen* | In a small company you have to pull your weight. |
| *auf eigenen Beinen stehen; auf sich allein gestellt sein* | When Tom left home he had to fend for himself. |
| *seinen Mann stehen; sich nicht unterkriegen lassen* | Even in difficult situations he had to keep his end up. |
| *ein Zimmer in der Chefetage bekommen* | Now he's a boss. He's got a room on the top floor. |
| *sich hocharbeiten* | Tom has certainly risen from the ranks. |
| *sich eine Karriere aufbauen* | Now John, his son, must carve his own career, too. |
| *auf eigenen Füßen stehen, selbständig sein* | John's already trying to paddle his own canoe. |

15

## LEVEL ⓜ

By profession I'm a trainer in industry. Sometimes I get the feeling it's like *throwing pearls before the swine* with some of these trainees. *You can lead a horse to water but you can't make him drink.* Anyway, through the training you have to be able to *separate the chaff from the grain.* And perhaps after two or three years you'll have an employee who is a *dab hand* at what he has to do.

### 1. Years of apprenticeship – *Lehrjahre*

| | |
|---|---|
| We've all got to start small. | *klein anfangen* |
| show someone the ropes | *jemandem die Regeln / Kniffe zeigen* |
| learn the hard way | *aus Erfahrung klug werden* |
| pass an exam with flying colours | *eine Prüfung mit Glanz und Gloria / fliegenden Fahnen bestehen* |
| get one's hand in | *sich eingewöhnen; vertraut werden mit; in Übung kommen* |
| keep one's hand in | *in Übung bleiben* |
| get the hang of something | *den richtigen Dreh finden; den Bogen rausbekommen* |
| Throw / cast pearls before swine. | *Perlen vor die Säue werfen.* |
| You can't make a silk purse out of a sow's ear. | *Aus einem Kieselstein kann man keinen Diamanten schleifen.* |
| You can lead a horse to water, but you can't make him drink. | *Mit Gewalt lässt sich (bei ihm / ihr) nichts erreichen.* |
| You can't teach an old dog new tricks. | *Was Hänschen nicht lernt, lernt Hans nimmermehr.* |

### QUICK CHECK 9: What's it in English?

Two apprentices:

**A:** Do you reckon this training is worth anything? As soon as you (*sich eingewöhnen*) they put you on a new job. Then you forget the other skill.

**B:** You're right, of course, but we've all (*klein anfangen müssen*). And then there's the question of the exams.

**A:** Yes, if you don't (*mit Glanz und Gloria bestehen*), you don't get taken on.

## 2. Filling a vacancy – *Eine Stelle besetzen*

| | |
|---|---|
| fill a vacancy | *eine freie Stelle / Posten besetzen* |
| contact a head-hunter | *einen Personalberater für die Suche nach Führungskräften kontaktieren* |
| be cut out for something | *für etwas wie geschaffen sein* |
| put to the test | *auf die Probe stellen* |
| be a hard nut to crack | *eine harte Nuss zu knacken geben* |
| not be up to the mark for the job | *nicht das Zeug für eine Stelle haben* |
| draw up a short list of applicants | *Bewerber in die engere Auswahl nehmen* |
| be on the short-list | *in der engeren Auswahl stehen* |
| offer a steady job | *sichere Arbeitsstelle anbieten* |
| mention the perks | *Leistungsanreize erwähnen* |
| seize the opportunity | *die Gelegenheit beim Schopf packen* |
| be a high-flier / shooting star | *ein Senkrechtstarter sein* |
| separate the sheep from the goats; separate the wheat from the chaff | *die Spreu vom Weizen trennen* |
| Good workers are far and few between. | *Gute Arbeiter sind spärlich gesät / wachsen nicht auf den Bäumen.* |

### QUICK CHECK 10: Let's go *woggling* again

Tony and Ron discuss Tom Dobson:

**T:** So you've appointed Dobson.
**R:** Yes, it was difficult to find anybody. We had to *contact a head-woggler.*
**T:** Well, I wouldn't have employed him. I don't think he's *up to the woggle.*
**R:** I know, but good workers are *far and few bewoggle*, so I took the risk. Maybe he's *woggled out for* this type of work.

## QUICK CHECK 11: What is it?

1. Some firms offer a car and free health insurance. These are typical .................................. .
2. Small number of candidates for a job, etc, selected from a larger number, and from which the successful candidate will be selected: draw up a ..................................
3. Be of the required standard: Be up ..................................

## 3. Good workers – *Gute Arbeiter*

| | |
|---|---|
| know the ins and outs of something | *etwas in- und auswendig kennen; etwas gründlich beherrschen* |
| know the score / all the angles | *alle Tricks / Kniffe genau kennen* |
| know one's onions / stuff | *sein Geschäft verstehen* |
| know the ropes | *den Bogen raushaben* |
| learn the ropes | *sich einarbeiten* |
| be the work horse of the company | *das Arbeitspferd der Firma sein* |
| bite the bullet and try one's best | *die Zähne zusammenbeißen und sein Bestes versuchen* |
| She dots the "i"s and crosses the "t"s. | *Sie erledigt ihre Aufgaben mit peinlicher Genauigkeit.* |
| be a dab hand at something | *ein goldenes Händchen bei etwas haben; etwas aus dem Effeff können* |
| be head and shoulders above the rest | *den anderen haushoch überlegen sein* |
| be snowed under with work | *bis zum Hals in Arbeit stecken* |
| have something at one's fingertips | *etwas aus dem Effeff beherrschen* |
| do the donkey work | *die mühselige Knochenarbeit machen* |
| work like a dog / horse | *wie ein Tier schuften; sich abrackern* |
| work one's fingers to the bone | *sich die Finger wund arbeiten* |
| be rushed / run off one's feet | *bis zum Umfallen arbeiten; kein Bein auf den Boden kriegen* |
| be the dog's body | *Mädchen für alles sein* |
| be up to one's eyes / neck in work | *bis zum Hals in Arbeit stecken; alle Hände voll zu tun haben* |

| | |
|---|---|
| be swamped with paperwork | *im Papierkram ersticken* |
| bite off more than one can chew | *sich zu viel vornehmen / zumuten* |
| speed things up | *Dampf dahinter machen; etwas vorantreiben* |
| not do anything by halves | *nicht auf halbem Wege stehen bleiben* |
| put one's back into it | *sich ins Zeug legen* |
| have got the hang of something | *den Dreh raushaben* |
| move heaven and earth | *alle Hebel in Bewegung setzen* |
| take it all in one's stride | *etwas spielend tun (schaffen)* |
| be involved heart and soul | *mit Leib und Seele dabei sein* |
| work around the clock | *rund um die Uhr arbeiten* |
| burn the midnight oil | *bis spät in die Nacht arbeiten* |
| work under someone's thumb | *unter jemandes Fuchtel arbeiten* |
| bend over backwards | *sich ein Bein ausreißen* |
| keep one's nose to the grindstone | *sich dahinter klemmen; schuften* |
| roll one's sleeves up | *die Ärmel hochkrempeln; in die Hände spucken* |
| pull out all the stops | *alle Register ziehen; alles dransetzen* |
| work hand in hand with someone | *mit jemandem Hand in Hand arbeiten* |
| praise someone to the skies | *über den grünen Klee loben / jemanden in den Himmel heben* |
| win one's spurs | *sich die Sporen verdienen* |

## TIME FOR A SMILE

"A return ticket please." – "Where to, sir?"
"Back here, please."

## QUICK CHECK 12: Body idioms

1. Tom's a dab .......................... at trouble-shooting computer problems.
2. He has data processing at his .......................... .
3. He's often up to his .......................... in work.
4. But he's always ready to work his .......................... to the bone.

## QUICK CHECK 13: What is the second part of the body?

1. Ron is involved heart and ........................... in his work.
2. They're head and ........................... above the rest.
3. And they work hand in ........................... with their partners.

## QUICK CHECK 14: Troubleshoot the idioms

Two colleagues talk about their work; Anita and Ortrud:

**O:** Well, you've been with us two years now. You certainly *wonk the pores.*
**A:** Yes, but it's difficult. I'm *sowned runed with work.*
**O:** I see it. And in some way you're treated as the *god's body*. Perhaps you should look for another job.
**A:** Oh, no. I'm happy here. I'll just *keep my neso to the stongerind* and it'll be alright.

### TIME FOR A SMILE

Traveller: "Excuse me, do you have a room for tonight?"
Hotel owner: "Certainly, sir. It'll be fifteen pounds a night. Or I can let you have a room for only five pounds, if you make your own bed."
Traveller: "I'll take the five-pound room."
Hotel owner: "Right I'll just go and fetch the wood, the hammer and the nails for the bed."

## 4. Bad workers – *Schlechte Arbeiter*

| | |
|---|---|
| He's not exactly killing himself. | *Er reißt sich nicht gerade ein Bein aus.* |
| be a lazy sod / lazybones | *faul wie die Sünde sein* |
| sleep till all hours | *bis in die Puppen schlafen* |
| sit back and take things easy | *die Hände in den Schoß legen* |
| be fed up to the back teeth with something; be sick of something | *zum Halse heraushängen; die Schnauze voll haben* |
| take something lightly | *auf die leichte Schulter nehmen* |
| have a cushy job | *eine ruhige Kugel schieben* |

| | |
|---|---|
| shelve something | *etwas auf die lange Bank schieben* |
| That's all double Dutch. | *Ich verstehe nur Bahnhof.* |
| start floundering | *ins Schwimmen kommen* |
| not move a muscle | *keinen Finger rühren* |
| set the fox to keep the geese | *den Bock zum Gärtner machen* |
| throw in the towel | *die Flinte ins Korn werfen* |
| drop a clanger | *einen Bock schießen* |
| let something slide | *etwas schleifen lassen* |
| He's a dead loss. | *Er ist ein totaler Versager.* |
| be fair to middling | *leidlich / so lala / mittelprächtig sein* |
| be all fingers and thumbs | *zwei linke Hände haben* |
| loaf around | *herumlungern* |
| have one's elevenses | *eine zweite Frühstückspause machen* |
| knock off work | *die Kelle fallen lassen* |
| be a millstone round the employer's neck | *ein Klotz am Bein des Arbeitgebers sein* |
| throw a spanner in the works | *Sand ins Getriebe streuen; einen Knüppel zwischen die Beine werfen* |
| break / smash something to smithereens | *etwas in tausend Stücke schlagen* |
| not know the first thing about something | *nicht die geringste Ahnung von etwas haben* |
| put the cart before the horse | *das Pferd vom Schwanz aufzäumen* |
| make heavy weather of something | *etwas beschwerlich / mühsam finden* |
| work at a snail's pace | *im Schneckentempo arbeiten* |
| not to lift a finger | *keinen Finger krumm machen* |
| not do a lick of work | *keinen Handschlag tun* |
| work to rule | *Dienst nach Vorschrift machen* |
| be on a go-slow | *Bummelstreik durchführen* |
| bite the hand that feeds you | *Undankbarkeit zeigen; Gutes mit Schlechtem vergelten* |
| not get one's hands dirty | *sich die Hände nicht schmutzig machen* |
| be on the dole | *stempeln gehen; arbeitslos sein* |
| sign on | *sich arbeitslos melden* |
| down tools | *die Arbeit niederlegen* |
| His heart is not in his work. | *Er ist mit dem Herz nicht bei der Sache.* |

15

## Time for a smile

A businessman visiting Brighton stopped at a hotel for an early evening drink. In the bar he got to know a very attractive girl. After a few drinks he took her over to the reception desk and booked a double room for the night, signing in as Mr and Mrs Doorbar. The next morning after breakfast he was presented with a bill for £950. "What's all this?" he exclaimed. "I've only been here one night, haven't I?"
"You're quite right, Mr Doorbar," said the clerk, "but your wife has been here for a week."

## QUICK CHECK 15: Animal idioms

1. If you appoint the wrong man for the job you set the ................ to keep the ................ .
2. Incompetent workers often put the cart before the ................ .
3. Lazybones tend to work at a ................'s pace.

## QUICK CHECK 16: Let's go *woggling* again

Union member and personnel manager:

**U:** We're not going to *woggle a muscle* to finish that job unless you discuss overtime with us again.
**P:** If you don't get on with it, you can all go and *woggle on.*
**U:** Are you threatening us? Okay lads, *down woggles!* Let's go and *have our woggles.*
**P:** It'll not be the last you hear of this. Don't *bite the woggle that feeds you!*

## 5. Firing – *Entlassen*

| | |
|---|---|
| give the push / sack / chop / bounce (sl) | *jemanden feuern / den Laufpass geben* |
| get the axe / boot (sl) | *gefeuert werden* |
| sack / fire / axe someone (sl) | *jemanden feuern / rauswerfen* |
| give someone a leaden handshake | *jemanden mit einer mageren Abfindung entlassen* |
| give an employee his cards / walking papers | *jemandem die Papiere geben / ihn entlassen* |
| be at a loose end | *beschäftigungslos sein; in der Luft hängen* |
| give notice to an employee | *einen Angestellten entlassen* |

## QUICK CHECK 17: Remember the idioms?

Managing Director and Personnel Manager on a difficult subject:

**M:** You want to give Johnson *the* ................? Are you sure it's the right decision?

**P:** We have to ................ *someone* and he's my first choice. He's a lazy so-and-so.

**M:** He's been here a long time. He'll have to get more than a l ............... *handshake.*

**P:** As far as I am concerned he could get a lead chain round his neck and off to the river with him.

**M:** Hey, careful now!

1

# CHAPTER 1

## QUICK CHECK 1:

| | |
|---|---|
| **1.** He was *born* in a clinic. | **2.** He was *christened* Boris. |
| **3.** He was *raised* by his grandma. | **4.** He *fell in* love with a girl. |
| **5.** He got *engaged.* | **6.** He got *married.* |
| **7.** He was *divorced.* | **8.** He fell *ill.* |
| **9.** He *died.* | **10.** He was *buried.* |

## QUICK CHECK 2: Find the rhyme

In the prime of his *life*
Boris met his future wife.
At the age of 70 Boris fell ill.
It was high time to make his *will.*

## QUICK CHECK 3: How to satisfy civil servants

Which documents do you need to make a civil servant believe that

| | |
|---|---|
| **1.** you were born? | *birth certificate* |
| **2.** you are not a citizen of Iraq? | *passport* |
| **3.** you are dead? | *death certificate* |

## QUICK CHECK 4: Civil servants ask these questions

| What was the question if this is | your answer? |
|---|---|
| **1.** What is your *sex*, sir? | *male* |
| **2.** What is your first name, sir? | *Boris* |
| **3.** What is your last name, sir? | *Baker* |
| **4.** What is your nationality, sir? | *German* |
| **5.** What is your age, sir? | *35* |
| **6.** What is your marital status? | *single* |

## QUICK CHECK 5: Baby idioms in business

1 D, 2 C, 3 A, 4 B

## QUICK CHECK 6: Idioms overheard

**B:** Damnation. That child has no *manners.* He should be disciplined.
**R:** Oh Bob, you were young *once* though I can't imagine it.
**B:** Very funny, but it doesn't change the fact that that little boy is *badly-brought up.* I tell you what I'd do with him ...

## QUICK CHECK 7: The early life of Boris

1. Boris was one of the baby *boom* generation.
2. At the age of six he was still in his *nappies.*
3. At the age of 14 he was at an *awkward / difficult* age.
4. At the age of 17 he started to *sow* his wild *oats.*
5. When he came of age he cut his *teeth* as a mechanic.
6. Today he designs robots. But they have a lot of *teething* problems.

## QUICK CHECK 8: Idioms overheard

**R:** You try to *carve* out a *career* and you get a smack an the nose.
**H:** I passed all my exams with *flying colours* and started working. And now after all these years I get *kicked upstairs.*

## QUICK CHECK 9: Can you speed-read?

1. Boris was born with a *silver spoon* in his mouth.
2. He could read when he was still in his *nappies.*
3. He became a *prefect* because he never played *truant.*
4. He tried to *paddle* his own *canoe* when he was still under age.

## QUICK CHECK 10: Idioms overheard

**C:** He *passed away quietly* while watching the TV. He didn't *suffer a painful end.*
**C:** It's true he was a bit *shaky on his feet*, but he never complained. And he *was getting long in the tooth*, after all he was almost eighty.

## QUICK CHECK 11: Odd man out

1 D, 2 C, 3 A

2

## CHAPTER 2

### QUICK CHECK 1: Find the noun

| | |
|---|---|
| be badly *wounded* | get a bad *wound* |
| be *injured* | have an *injury* |
| be *bleeding* | blood is *running* down |
| *bandage* a wound | put on a *bandage* |

### QUICK CHECK 2: Health in figures

**What does the doctor call these measurements?**

| | |
|---|---|
| number of heartbeats | *pulse rate* |
| blood and fat | *cholesterol level* |
| arteries and pressure | *blood pressure* |

### QUICK CHECK 3: Find just the right verb

| | |
|---|---|
| *go* | on a diet |
| *catch* | a cold |
| *damage* | one's health |
| *give* | someone an injection |
| *recover* | one's strength |
| *suffer* | from headaches |
| *give* | someone relief |

### QUICK CHECK 4: Which doctor do you go to if ...

1. you are pregnant? *gynaecologist*
2. you have a stomach ulcer? *surgeon*
3. you've had a cough for weeks? *ear, nose and throat specialist*

### QUICK CHECK 5: Correct the typical German mistakes

1. Tom was *taken* to hospital.
2. He is in intensive care.
3. He will be operated *on* tomorrow.

## QUICK CHECK 6: Correct the typical German mistakes



1. Where is the *nearest* chemist?
2. For these pills you need a *prescription* from your doctor.
3. I wish you a *speedy* recovery.

## QUICK CHECK 7: Idioms overheard

P: How was your trip to Italy? I must say you *look a picture of health.*

S: I was a bit sick before I went, but I *shook it off* after two or three days. Now I'm *feeling like a million dollars.*

## QUICK CHECK 8: Idioms overheard

At the doctors, doctor and Bob:

B: Doctor, I feel completely *run-down.* I even *feel giddy*. My *head starts to spin.*

D: You've *been burning the candle at both ends.* That's why you *feel out of sorts.*

B: Give me some ideas how I can *recharge my batteries.*

## QUICK CHECK 9: Can you speed-read this?

R: I didn't *sleep a wink* last night.

A: I must say you *look all tuckered out.* Listen, you *grab forty winks* and I'll finish off this chapter.

R: I think I'll take a week off before I *conk out* completely. Is that okay with you?

## QUICK CHECK 10: Find the mistakes

Doctor and nurse in a hospital:

D: Quick, nurse, pass me the oxygen. This patient is *within an inch of losing his life.*

N: He does look bad. We thought he was going to be all right, but that pneumonia *was the final nail in his coffin.*

D: Never mind! If we don't act quickly he won't *be long for this world.* Let's do our best.

3

## CHAPTER 3

### QUICK CHECK 1: Tim, the yes-man

**Tom:** What would you advise me? Shall I *take Tina out* tonight?
**Tim:** Yes, Tom, if I were you I'd *wine and dine her.*
**Tom:** What about the Red Lion? They do good *local meals* there.
**Tim:** Yes, they do very good *local cuisine.*
**Tom:** Should I *reserve* a table?
**Tim:** *Yes, if I were you I'd book* a table.

### QUICK CHECK 2: Understanding the menu

| | | |
|---|---|---|
| 2 | The meat of a pig | pork |
| 3 | The meat of a baby cow | veal |
| 4 | The meat of a deer | venison |
| 5 | Mussels or lobster | seafood |

### QUICK CHECK 3: What to say to the waiter

You want ...

| | | |
|---|---|---|
| 1 | the list with the meals: | Could *I have the menu*, please? |
| 2 | to choose the wine: | Could *I have the wine list*, please? |
| 3 | to tell the waiter your choice: | Could *you take my order*, please? |

### QUICK CHECK 4: Find the chronological order

4 Last orders. Please!
3 I'm full.
1 And the vegetables?
5 Time, Ladies and Gentlemen, please.
2 And to follow?

## QUICK CHECK 5: Is it true ore false?

| | True | False |
|---|---|---|
| 1. The sweet is the dessert. | ✔ | |
| 2. Venison is a green salad. | | ✔ |
| 3. Wild boar is a vegetarian dish. | | ✔ |
| 4. The menu is made of paper. | ✔ | |
| 5. Low-cholesterol dishes are low-fat dishes. | ✔ | |
| 6. A second helping is the same as a second spoon. | | ✔ |

## QUICK CHECK 6: The chef's mistakes

1. I wanted my steak (**B.**) well-done.
2. Green beans should be (**C.**) well-cooked.
3. Waiter, why don't you serve the potatoes (**A.**) boiled?

## QUICK CHECK 7: Beautiful people

Everybody, *let's celebrate* her beauty with a glass of champagne.
*Here is to* the charming bride.
And I also want to *wish* you and Steve *the best of luck* ...

## QUICK CHECK 8: You'd better go on the wagon

Annette and Ron discuss his problems:

**A:** Why *have you taken to drink* again? What's happened?
**R:** I *hit the bottle* after we got the company results. Yesterday *I painted the town red*. And now I've *got a hangover*.
**A:** Well, I'm not surprised. It serves you right.

## QUICK CHECK 9: Get the idioms right

After the jog. Bob and Sue:

**B:** That was twenty kilometres. But now I could *murder a steak.*
**S:** Wait a minute! Think of the *weight you'll put on*. The jog will be wasted.
**B:** Well, look at all the food you *cram down your throat* and you never put any weight on.
**S:** No, but you do!

3

## QUICK CHECK 10: Body idioms

1. The delicious smell from the kitchen made my *mouth water.*
2. And I could eat caviar and oysters to my *heart's content.*
3. There was a T-bone steak that would *stick* to my *ribs.*
4. Anne knew that I have a *sweet tooth*. The desert was second to none.
5. I hope you aren't going to eat her *head* off.

## QUICK CHECK 11: The choice is yours

**B:** He's *having* [**A.**] *forty winks.*
**R:** When did he *hit the* [**B.**] *sack*?
**B:** But he's been *sleeping like a* [**C.**] *log* ever since.
**R:** Okay, let's leave him to *sleep it* [**A.**] *off.*

## QUICK CHECK 12: Remember the idiom?

1. go on the wagon
2. take a hair of the dog that bit one
3. wet one's whistle
4. wolf down something

## CHAPTER 4



### QUICK CHECK 1: Complete the comparisons

1. Tom is as broad as a *barn.*
2. He's as strong as an *ox.*
3. Unfortunately he's as ugly as *sin.*

### QUICK CHECK 2: A question of size

1. He's a bit on the *short* side.
2. She's already very *tall* for her age.
3. Napoleon was a *short* man, but a *great* leader.

### QUICK CHECK 3: What's the opposite?

| | |
|---|---|
| When he was young Tim had a fine head of hair. | Today he's as *bald* as a coot. |
| Sue has a natural wave in her hair. | Tina gets her hair *permed* every two months. |
| She wears it long and curly. | Anne has got short and *straight* hair. |

### QUICK CHECK 4: Describe these noses

| | | | |
|---|---|---|---|
|  | a *hooked* nose | 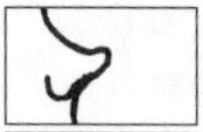 | a nice *turned-up* nose |
|  | a *snub* nose |  | a *pointed* nose. |

### QUICK CHECK 5: Bob and Ron are different

| | |
|---|---|
| Bob always looks *pale.* | Ron has a good *suntan.* |
| Bob doesn't dress *well.* | Ron is always in *fashion.* |
| Bob only buys *off the peg.* | All Ron's suits are *tailor-made.* |
| Bob' face is *angular.* | Ron's face is *round.* |

## QUICK CHECK 6: Four mistakes to correct

**R:** Did you see that woman who came for an interview this morning? She's *the spitting image of* Lucy Bruhn.

**S:** Actually, she's Lucy's younger sister. They *are as like as two peas in a pod.* And they both *take after their mother.*

**R:** Well, I hope the new girl works as hard as her sister.

## QUICK CHECK 7: Fill them in

Two clerks talk about the company doctor:

**P:** And the doctor asked me when I last drank wine. I couldn't *keep my face straight.*

**J:** What did you tell him that? You drink more than a bottle every day.

**P:** I told him. He *gave me filthy look.*

**J:** Well, be careful. You could ruin your liver. Then you'll *have egg on your face.*

## QUICK CHECK 8: Remember the idioms?

1. When the department leader read out a complaint the hot-line clerk *went as red as a beetroot.*
2. Ron told Tom his work was not good enough. Tom wasn't interested and *turned his nose up* at Ron.
3. Okay, she's left you and it's difficult. Never mind, you've got to *keep a stiff upper lip* in any case.

## QUICK CHECK 9: Bob and Ron are different

**R:** You've jogged more than ten kilometres. Don't exaggerate. You're already *as thin as a rake.*

**B:** You should jog, too. You *cut a sorry figure.*

**R:** I've been doing sports since I *was knee-high to a grasshopper.*

**R:** And you're still hopping around with all your injuries.

## QUICK CHECK 10: What's the *woggle*?

**J:** My goodness, you're *all spruced up*. Have you got a job interview or what?
**S:** No, I haven't actually. I've got a dinner date.
**J:** Well, you *stick out like a sore thumb* here at work. And by the way, that sort of dress *is a bit out of fashion.*
**S:** Jean, you *are* really *behind the times.*

## QUICK CHECK 11: Take a vowel for an x

Director of personnel and personnel manager talk about age:

**D:** So now you're sixty. I know *you're* not at all *past it,* but you have to think about your pension.
**P:** You're right. I'm beginning to *feel my age.*
**D:** Well, you're *getting a bit long in the tooth.* No, that's a joke. Of course it's the same for me. *I'm pushing fifty* as well.

## QUICK CHECK 12: Only one is correct

1. Young Tom is a chip of the old block. He and his father are both (**B.**) cast in the same mould.
2. Tom and his brother, however, are (**A.**) as different as chalk and cheese
3. Ron has lost 20 kilos. He's now (**C.**) as thin as a rake.
4. When he realized that he had lost a lot of money at the stock exchange he knew (**A.**) he had egg on his face.
5. He tried to sell me this yellow suit. He said that (**C.**) it fitted me like a glove.

## CHAPTER 5

### QUICK CHECK 1: Tim, the yes man

1. Do you trust Tom? – Yes, he is very *trustworthy.*
2. Bob showed great courage when he arrested the gangster. – Yes, he was very *courageous.*
3. I believe in his sincerity – Yes, he's completely *sincere.*
4. He's known for his generosity. – Yes, he's very *generous.*

### QUICK CHECK 2: Incompatible characters

1. Bob has a *strong* character. His brother has a *weak* character.
2. Susan is very *punctual*. Her colleague is always *late.*
3. Bob is an *open character.* His wife is very *reserved.*
4. Bob works *efficiently.* Brian is a *lazy* fellow.

### QUICK CHECK 3: Let's characterise them!

1 E, 2 C, 3 D, 4 A, 5 B

### QUICK CHECK 4: Get to know yourself

1. If you spend too much you're *careless with* money.
2. If you torture cats and dogs you're *cruel to* animals.
3. If you never work overtime you're a *lazy* fellow.
4. If you behave badly at table you have *no manners.*

### QUICK CHECK 5: Silly questions about Betsy and Bert

| | |
|---|---|
| 1. She wouldn't say *boo* to a goose. | She's harmless, gentle. |
| 2. *Butter* wouldn't melt in her mouth. | She is absolutely innocent. |
| 3. Tom wears his heart on his *sleeve.* | He's in love. |
| 4. His *bark* is worse that his bite. | He's a rough diamond, but not a bad sort. |

## QUICK CHECK 6: Fit these animals in

**R:** He deceived us once. He's *as slippery as an eel.*

**A:** Right, and when he first presented himself you would *have thought you could read him like an open book.* Anyway I had the feeling *he was a bit of a cold fish.*

**R:** And to cancel all his courses by pretending he was in hospital. *What a snake in the grass!*

## QUICK CHECK 7: What's the woggle?

**R:** It's too late *to learn the ins and outs* of a country, of its systems.

**A:** Well, you wouldn't, would you? One has to be quick on the *uptake* or you'll make mistakes.

**R:** Don't worry! Change and risk, *that's my middle name.*

## QUICK CHECK 8: Remember the animal idioms?

1. There are *no flies on him.*
2. She *took to it like a duck to water.*
3. He's as *crafty as a fox.*

## QUICK CHECK 9: Fill the gaps

The handyman. Bob and Ron discuss him:

**B:** So, I'm absolutely furious. My new plumber is as blind as a *bat* and he's *bone-idle* too.

**R:** Bob, I warned you not to employ him. It was so clear to me that he wouldn't do a *stroke* of work. Poor old Bob. There's one *born* every minute.

## QUICK CHECK 10: Tim, the yes-man

Is Bert the right man?

1. Yes, you can't *teach an old dog new tricks*.
2. Yes, he seems to have *bats in his belfry*.
3. Yes, he'll *turn out to be a turkey*, as the Americans say.
4. Yes, he's a *parasite on* the company.

# CHAPTER 6

## QUICK CHECK 1: Think & Co

1. I'm not interested in buying a house. What made you *think of* that?
2. This house is really a good bargain. *Think* it *over.*
3. One should *think* twice *about* before buying a house.

## QUICK CHECK 2: Translation exercise

**B:** *After some thought* I've decided not to meet Oro's deadlines.

**R:** *Believe it or not*, I absolutely agree with you. And I'd like to add that *they must be out of their senses / have taken leave of their senses* setting such short deadlines.

**B:** For me *it's only common sense* to have a bit more time ...

## QUICK CHECK 3: More of Ron's opinion

Well, I'm pretty *convinced* that if they attack this country it means that all over the world reasonable, moderate Muslims will take sides with the extremists. *As I see it* the West should only make targeted attacks against the terrorists. *If you ask me* some Americans *aren't at all aware of* the dangers we're facing.

## QUICK CHECK 4: Beef up your word power

1. It's my firm *belief* that he is not the right man.
2. Yes, it is my *conviction*, too, that we'd regret it .
3. I've already made the *decision*. I'm going to cancel this post altogether.

## QUICK CHECK 5: Silly questions

1. What can two people do with an opinion? They can *share* it.
2. What can you have if you disagree? You can have some *reservations.*
3. How do you see it if you don't agree? You see it a little *differently.*

## QUICK CHECK 6: Is it mind or memory?

1. I can't get the bank robbery out of my *mind.*
2. The police showed me photos to jog my *memory.*
3. Normally I've got a good *memory* for faces.
4. But after a night with Sue I was not of sound *mind* and *memory.*
5. I wasn't able to describe the bank robber from *memory.*
6. I just couldn't call his face to *mind.*

## QUICK CHECK 7: What to do with his brain / mind

1. *pick someone's brains*
   to question someone who knows a lot about something in order to obtain information
2. *rack one's brains*
   to try very hard to think of something or remember something
3. *have something on one's mind*
   to think about something all the time and be unable to forget it even if one wants to.

## QUICK CHECK 8: Repair the idioms

1. That's all *Greek* to me!
2. It's all double *Dutch* to me.
3. I'm not exactly an *Einstein.*

## QUICK CHECK 9: What's the *woggle*?

Anita is talking about her estranged husband:

**R:** *Penny for your thoughts.* What's in your head?
**A:** Oh, it's nothing really. I was *toying with the idea of* getting a new flat.
**R:** Sounds great. When?
**A:** Well, it depends on my husband. He's *having second thoughts* about our relationship.
**R:** Hey, Anita! *Have you got a screw loose*? You've got to live your own life. Don't give him a second thought.

## QUICK CHECK 10: What's the *woggle*?

Melissa is thinking about her arrival in Heidelberg.

It's really strange. As I walked down High Street I had the feeling I'd been here before. *It came to my mind* that I'd sat somewhere here in a little wine pub with a friend of mine. But *it's slipped my mind* who I was with. For some reason I can't remember. It's *as if my memory has been wiped clean.* Still, never mind. It'll come back to me later.

## QUICK CHECK 11: Translation exercise

**B:** When will the Green Party *nail their colours to the mast* and say whether they support the USA in its war against terrorism.

**S:** Yes, it's high time they took a *firm / tough stand on* that issue.

**B:** They are still quarrelling among themselves and we're waiting to see *which side of the fence they come down on.*

**S:** *You can wait till the cows come home*! You know what they are like.

## CHAPTER 7



### QUICK CHECK 1: Words plus prepositions

You know that I'm not *keen on* going on a holiday with Tom, at all.
I'd *hoped for* more: Italy, Spain or Portugal. I don't *care for* a holiday in Germany, least of all in Gelsenkirchen.
Tom, on the other hand, *disapproves of* long, expensive trips. And he's very *fond of* historic coalmines and things like that.

### QUICK CHECK 2: Same meaning

| | |
|---|---|
| I can't *stand* optimists. | I can't *bear* optimists. |
| ... there's no *reason* to *be alarmed.* | ... there's no *need* to *worry.* |
| But there's always a reason to be *concerned* about something. | But there's always a reason to be *worried* about something. |
| Tonight I'll *frighten* Tom to death ... | Tonight I'll *scare* Tom to death ... |

### QUICK CHECK 3: What the priest shouted to the passengers

1. Keep your [A.] *hair* on.
2. Don't lose your [C.] *heads.*
3. Don't lose hope! [B.] *Chin up*, we'll be rescued.
4. You should [B.] *cheer up.* Where there's life, there's hope.

### QUICK CHECK 4: What's the opposite

| | |
|---|---|
| Everything is going *well* today. | Nothing is going *right* today. |
| Things could be *better.* | Things could be *worse.* |
| Look on the *bright* side. | Look on the *black* side. |

### QUICK CHECK 5: What's the *woggle*?

1. Since he left her, my secretary's been sitting at her desk *crying* her *eyes* out.
2. She's stopped crying now, but I can see that she's *eating* her heart out.
3. She's physically and mentally on her last *legs* – we'll have to look for a new secretary.

## QUICK CHECK 6: Fill in the missing letters

1. I'm really *in the doldrums.* I haven't got the money.
2. I *felt really cheap.*
3. I'm really *at my wits' end.*

## QUICK CHECK 7: Churchyard idioms

1. There was the *devil* to pay when we got home that night.
2. Aunt Augusta went as *white* as a *sheet* when we suddenly appeared in the living room. The guests left in a hurry.
3. "You're the *last nail in my coffin,*" she shouted at us and the knife gleamed in the candlelight.
4. The sight of the knife *gave me the creeps.*

## QUICK CHECK 8: xs for vowels

I was walking home last night when suddenly a man jumped out of the bushes. I was *scared stiff.* And he looked so aggressive. I was *shaking like a leaf*, but I pulled myself together. "What do you want?" I bellowed. "Nothing mate, I've just had too much to drink." And he ran off. But I must say, I had *got goose pimples.*

## QUICK CHECK 9: Idioms from the kitchen

1. Instead of discussing the problem with his son, Tom *bottled* up all his anger.
2. When he heared that Tom wanted to marry Susan, a prostitute, he flipped his *lid.*
3. When Tom learned that Susan already had two children he popped his *cork.*

## QUICK CHECK 10: Translation exercise

Anthony and Ron discuss Lorry, a former trainer:

**A:** So, she's going. I didn't expect it. *That's the last straw*! It's all the fault of this law.

**R:** Well, I must say I *lost my cool* when I heard the news. Actually I *flew into a rage / threw a fit / threw a tantrum.*

## CHAPTER 8



### QUICK CHECK 1: Those pesky prepositions

1. I've taken a fancy *to* animals.
2. My wife , too, has a great love *for* animals.
3. We're very fond *of* our two dogs.
4. We get a lot of pleasure *out of* playing with them.

### QUICK CHECK 2: Beef up your word power

Say it with the noun.

| | |
|---|---|
| Anna *was relieved* when we left. | She sighed with *relief* when we left. |
| Jim *prefers* Italian wines to German ones. | He has a *preference* for Italian wines. |
| We were *pleased* to hear Jim sing. | It is always a *pleasure* listening to Jim sing. |

### QUICK CHECK 3: What's the woggle?

1. I was *looking* forward *to* going to Jim's party.
2. I was *grateful* that I had been invited.
3. All the guests arrived at the party in high *spirits.*
4. It was a wonderful party and we *enjoyed* ourselves very much.
5. Everybody was in the seventh *heaven.*

### QUICK CHECK 4: Spot the mistake

1. Old Dunbar was looking forward to *being* a grandfather.
2. He was keen to *be* the first to congratulate Joe and Sue.
3. He was eager *to see* the newly born babies.
4. He gets a lot of pleasure *from* his grandchildren.

## QUICK CHECK 5: Knowing what's what

| | |
|---|---|
| an expression of the face showing happiness, amusement or pleasure | *smile* |
| make the sounds and movements of the face and body that express amusement | *laugh* |
| smile widely, especially with the mouth open | *grin* |
| laugh quietly to oneself. | *chuckle* |
| low unpleasant laugh, especially at something rude or at another person's troubles. | *snigger* |

## QUICK CHECK 6: Beware of false friends

1. Tina doesn't know I'm in love with her. (**C.**) head over heels
2. She told me she doesn't hate me. That's a weight from my (**A.**) shoulders.
3. I'm happy as a (**C.**) sandboy / lark.
4. I'll tell her that I love her and we'll both be on (**A.**) cloud nine

## QUICK CHECK 7: Remember the idioms?

**P:** Wow Jenny, I think Ron has got a *crush on you.* He's really staring at you.
**J:** Oh, that's not true. He's *walking on air* at the moment because he's just passed his university degree.
**P:** Oh, has he? With a degree, *the sky's the limit for him*, that's true enough.

## QUICK CHECK 8: Parts of the body

1. Bill was the life and *soul* of the party.
2. After the first drink he let his *hair* down.
3. And he pulled all the girls' *legs.*

## QUICK CHECK 9: What's the *woggle*?

**B:** I didn't like him when I first met him, but he's certainly *the life and soul of the party.*

**N:** You can say that again. And everybody seems to be *having a ball.*

**B:** But I don't feel very relaxed myself.

**N:** I noticed that. You don't seem able to *get a kick out of* anything. Try this pill.

## QUICK CHECK 10: Complete the idioms

1. *laugh up one's* sleeve
2. *grin like a Cheshire* cat
3. *have a laugh at someone's* expense

## QUICK CHECK 11: Silly questions

1. What did he laugh off? He laughed his *head* off.
2. What did he burst with laughter? He burst his *sides* with laughter.
3. Which side of his face did he laugh at? He laughed *at the other side* of his face.

## QUICK CHECK 12: What's the *woggle*?

**B:** You've got no sense of humour. When someone tells a funny joke you *keep a straight face.* When there's nothing to laugh about you *split your sides laughing.*

**N:** It's no good *braying with laughter* when other people are suffering. I'm just not willing to do that.

9

## CHAPTER 9

### QUICK CHECK 1: Beef up your word power

| | |
|---|---|
| I was *astonished* when I saw Tina with another man. | To my *astonishment* Liz took off all her clothes. |
| It was *surprised* te meet Joe in Berlin. | Is that you, Al? What a *surprise*! I haven't seen you for ages. |
| You'd be *amazed* to see what the robot is able to do. | To my *amazement* the robot began to speak. |

### QUICK CHECK 2: Find the mistakes

1. He stood *aghast* at the sight of Joe's ghost.
2. That was a *shot* from out of the blue.
3. It came as a *shock* for all of us.
4. He, too, seemed taken *aback* that we had recognized her.

### QUICK CHECK 3: Decisions! Decisions!

1. Suddenly I saw Joe. That was a shot from the [**C.**] *blue.*
2. He had survived. It's a [**C.**] *near-miracle.*
3. That can't be true. Go and [**A.**] *tell it* to the marines.
4. I can't get [**B.**] *over* it.

### QUICK CHECK 4: What's the *woggle*?

**R:** He *dropped a real bombshell* about Phil, our former teacher.
**T:** Well, *that's a turn-up for the books.*

### QUICK CHECK 5: Take a vowel for an x

**R:** They've reduced interest rates by one percent. It *took me completely unawares.*
**A:** Yes. I know. That decision *came from out of the blue,* but it's great for us anyway.
**R:** That's right. We'll be able to save. And not before time. I *was completely floored* when I lost my job.

## QUICK CHECK 6: Odd man

**1. C.** Are you damned?
**2. B.** Great sky!
**3. C.** Holy crows!

## QUICK CHECK 7: Beef up your word power

Jack meets Alex in the middle of the jungle:

**J:** *Well, blow me / I'll be blowed*! What are you doing here?
**A:** *What the devil / hell* are you doing here?
**A:** *Are you joking / kidding*? In the depths of the jungle?

# CHAPTER 10

## QUICK CHECK 1: What's the opposite

| | |
|---|---|
| be the born *winner* | be the born *loser* |
| expect the *best* | expect the *worst* |
| born under a *lucky* star | born under an *unlucky* star |
| bet on the *right* horse | bet on the *wrong* horse |

## QUICK CHECK 2: Colourful phrases

1. Always look on the *bright* side of life.
2. He sees everything *black.*
3. He saw everything through *rose*-coloured glasses.

## QUICK CHECK 3: Violent phrases

1. Bankruptcy came as a heavy *blow* for Ron.
2. But lightning never *strikes* twice.
3. In November 2001 Ron *hit* the jackpot.
4. It was a *stroke* of luck.

## QUICK CHECK 4: Your choice

1. Das war fünf Minuten vor zwölf. **B.** That was the eleventh hour!
2. Ron ist noch mal davongekommen. **A.** That was a close shave.
3. Er hat den Vogel wieder mal abgeschossen. **A.** He took the cake again.

## QUICK CHECK 5: Silly questions

| | |
|---|---|
| **1.** Where should you always land? | on your *feet* |
| **2.** What should you knock on! | on *wood* |
| **3.** What should you always keep up? | your *pecker* |
| **4.** What does fortune favour? | It favours *fools.* |

## QUICK CHECK 6: Something went wrong here

**A:** I think you *bit off more than you can chew* with those courses.

**R:** Well, I had to try. I hadn't expected so much bad luck. *It never rains but it pours.*

**A:** I had *a run of bad luck last* year too, but you just have to keep your head down and *hope for the best.*

## QUICK CHECK 7: Tim, the 'yes-man'

**Tim:** Hard *cheese*, indeed!

**Tim:** We've got sweet *Fanny Adams.*

**Tim:** We haven't got a *snowball's* chance in *hell.*

## QUICK CHECK 8: What's the *woggle*?

Ron discusses the financial situation with Michael, his tax advisor:

**R:** I'm still hanging on by *the skin of my teeth.* But it's not easy.

**M:** As we say in Munich, "Where there's beer, there's hope". *You have to take the rough with the smooth.*

**R:** It's easy for you to say that, but I've been taking the rough with the rough for too long.

**M:** *Every cloud has a silver lining.*

**R:** But it's nothing but rain and storms at the moment.

## DOUBLE CHECK 9: Body idioms

1. I can feel it in my *bones.*
2. Don't let the opportunity slip right through your *fingers.*
3. That's easy when you're born with a silver spoon in your *mouth.*
4. Try to always land on your *feet.*
5. Keep your *fingers* crossed for me, mother!
6. Keep your *pecker* up!
7. Put a bold *face* on it!
8. Keep your *hair* on!
9. He escaped by the skin of his *teeth.*
10. Don't lose *heart*!

# CHAPTER 11

## QUICK CHECK 1: Typical German

1. We met *each other* at Frank's dinner party two years ago.
2. I'm also good *friends* with his wife, which makes problems.
3. I *got* to know her better after she had drunk a few beers.
4. His wife *divorced* Tony but they parted as friends.

## QUICK CHECK 2: Those nasty little words

1. I'm good friends *with* Tony's wife.
2. We weren't exactly the best *of* friends.
3. When she divorced him they parted *as* friends.
4. He's still *on* friendly terms *with* her.
5. Having a friend *in* Tony helped me to survive a crisis.

## QUICK CHECK 3: What's the woggle?

1. My son, Tom, *got carried away by* Yvette, our new au-pair girl.
2. He's absolutely *crazy about* the girl.
3. He feels like he's *walking on air* since he met Yvette.
4. Tom *proposed to* Yvette yesterday. They are *getting engaged* on Tuesday.

## QUICK CHECK 4: Body idioms

1. Tony was always willing to give me a *hand.*
2. Tom asked for Yvette's *hand* in marriage.
3. John's *head* over *heels* in love with her.

## QUICK CHECK 5: Idioms with a p

1. The new boss is *palling up with* his female employees.
2. She deserves a *pat on the back* for all the hard work she's done.
3. Would you please *put* in a good word for me with the boss?
4. You have to *pull strings* if you want to be successful in business.

## QUICK CHECK 6: What a mess!

S: We've known each other a long time. How long have we been *hanging out together?*

J: More than ten years. And we've been *getting on like a house on fire.*
S: Right, but now we've got a problem. I think you've been *cosying up* to my boyfriend.
J: It's the other way round. He's *currying favour with* me.

## QUICK CHECK 7: Remember the idioms?

| | |
|---|---|
| touch his / her feet lightly with one's own feet, usually under a table, as an expression of sexual interest | *play footsie with someone* |
| to live together when not married | *shack up with someone* |
| to look at someone in a loving but foolish way | *make sheep's eyes at someone* |
| make oneself seem more attractive, by not immediately accepting an invitation | *play hard to get* |

## QUICK CHECK 8: Going all the way

**R:** So you've *made a pass* at Maria?
**F:** Not really, but I guess I *turned on the old charm* a bit.
**R:** You *pick someone up* and you're always successful.
**F:** *I could drink her bathwater.*

## QUICK CHECK 10: Take a vowel for a ♥

Tom told me he's *gone a bundle on* Lara, a young girl from Poland. He said he's never met anyone like that and he was completely *hooked on* her. Well, Tom always was a bit impressionable; he's so young! But in a way he's a bit naïve. He thinks *life is a bed of roses* and doesn't see that some people are down in the dumps. Anyway, never mind, he's *walking on air*, at least for the time being.

## QUICK CHECK 11: Body idioms

1. "Well done!" he said and patted him on the *back.*
2. Tom tries to rub *shoulders* with the rich people of the town.
3. I found him to be *hand* in glove with my worst enemy.
4. He is a boy after my own *heart.*
5. Have you noticed, Tim is giving Sue the glad *eye*?
6. He seems to expect to be waited on *hand* and *foot.*

## CHAPTER 12

### QUICK CHECK 1: Which one is wrong?

1. **C.** I *can't support my family* – Ich kann meine Familie nicht unterstützen
2. **A.** You may *disagree* ... Sie mögen anderer Meinung sein ...
3. **D.** I *object to* all forms of violence – Ich bin gegen alle Formen von Gewalt

### QUICK CHECK 2: Beef up your word power

| | |
|---|---|
| 1. You deeply *offended* me. | I didn't mean any *offence.* |
| 2. Don't start *insulting* me. | It wasn't an *insult*, it was a compliment. |
| 3. I was *disgusted* with the way you behaved towards Anne. | Why should my behaviour fill you with *disgust.* |

### QUICK CHECK 3: Letter mix-up

1. He's always trying to *cheat people.*
2. He always *deceived* his wife.
3. He *treats the truth lightly.*

### QUICK CHECK 4: Phrases with a p

1. I gave one of them a *prod / push*
2. He *punched* my nose.
3. Then I beat him to a *pulp.*

### QUICK CHECK 5: Fill them in

1. I'm very disappointed. I have always trusted him and now he's trying to *stick a knife in my back.*
2. *I've got a bone to pick with you.* Where's the money I left on the kitchen table?
3. Doesn't he make you feel physically uncomfortable? – He *sets my teeth on edge* as soon as he enters the room.

## QUICK CHECK 6: What's it in English?

**J:** I really don't know what's wrong. I met Liz yesterday and I got the feeling *she has it in for me.*

**T:** What have you done to her? Maybe she wants to *get even with you* for something you've done.

**J:** I can't remember anything. Maybe it's something I said.

**T:** Yes, you're sometimes a bit tactless. But I must say Liz is *an awkward customer*, too.

**J:** Well, there's certainly *no love lost between* us.

## QUICK CHECK 7: It's your choice again

1. Ron is completely under Anne's control: She's got him under her (**A.**) thumb.
2. The way she acts makes it difficult for him to proceed with the project. She is cutting (**A.**) the ground from under his feet.
3. She knew all along that Ron had a girlfriend and was laughing up (**C.**) her sleeve at Ron.

## QUICK CHECK 8: What's the *woggle*?

Ron and Bryan talk about Peter whom they've just met in the pub.

**R:** Well, Pete's not changed much. He's still *slagging people off* behind their backs.

**B:** You're right there. He's always *got his knife into someone* or another.

**R:** One of these days somebody will get to know what he's saying and then they'll *settle the score* with him. And it'll serve him right.

## QUICK CHECK 9: Body idioms

1. Stop being so critical. You always cut down Anita to the *bone*.
2. You're always hurting everybody's feelings. Be more reserved and don't put Anita's *nose* out of joint all the time.
3. And stop telling everybody how you would run the country. Nobody likes having your extremist ideas forced down their *throats*.

12

## QUICK CHECK 10: Let's go *woggling* again

**B:** I'll give him *a black eye* if he keeps staring.

**R:** My God, you're drunk. Look, that big fellow's coming over. Watch out or we'll be *having a barney.*

**B:** I couldn't care less. I'll *give him hell* if he comes near me.

**S:** Hey, *them's fighting words*. Take your glasses off.

## QUICK CHECK 11: More silly questions

You will ...

1. pour *oil* on troubled waters
2. hold out the *olive* branch to your partner
3. bury the *hatchet*

## QUICK CHECK 12: A vowel for an x

**R:** Now then, Sid, you're *getting the wrong end of the stick.*

**S:** You must be joking. He was threatening me.

**R:** He's just a bit drunk. He's only *getting it out of his system.*

**S:** Let's *put something straight*. If he does that again, I'll bop him.

## CHAPTER 13



### QUICK CHECK 1: What a mess!

1. I was *chatting* with some ladies.
2. I wanted to tell them the *story* of my *life*.
3. I need to *explain* my problems to them.
4. I'll *mention* that I won at the horse races.
5. I'll just *drop* a *hint* that I'm a very rich man.

### QUICK CHECK 2: Beef up your word power

| noun | verb |
|---|---|
| description | *describe* |
| repetition | *repeat* |
| advice | *advise* |
| suggestion | *suggest* |
| promise | *promise* |

### QUICK CHECK 3: Word power the other way round

| verb | noun |
|---|---|
| inform | *information* |
| inquire | *inquiry* |
| repeat | *repetition* |
| recommend | *recommendation* |
| confess | *confession* |

### QUICK CHECK 4: Ways of speaking

1. *shout*
2. *argue*
3. *whisper*

## QUICK CHECK 5: A letter mix to sort out

1. First I heard loud *yells of rage.*
2. Then one of the men *cried out in pain.*
3. After a few minutes his *screams* became fainter.

## QUICK CHECK 6: Silly questions

| | |
|---|---|
| 1. What is golden? | *silence* |
| 2. What can you sometimes hear drop? | *a pin* |
| 3. Where do some people take their secrets? | *into the grave* |
| 4. What speak louder than words? | *actions* |

## QUICK CHECK 7: What's the woggle?

**B:** Didn't you get an appointment with the Chairman of the Board?

**R:** Next week. But at present my customer **is** *keeping its own counsel.* They're saying nothing.

**B:** I think they're trying to *keep the lid on* their own bad management.

**R:** You're probably right. But that doesn't help. I need to know things. In this situation *silence* certainly *is not golden.*

## QUICK CHECK 8: What can you do with brick walls?

1. You can *bang* your head against a brick wall trying to achieve something impossible.
2. Sometimes people, especially teachers have to *talk* to a brick wall.
3. Some journalists think they can *see* through a brick wall.

## QUICK CHECK 9: Remember the idioms?

Boyfriend problems, Bob and Ron.

**B:** So Steffi's got a new boyfriend. It's terrible. She *hangs on his every word.*

**R:** You mean she doesn't listen to you any more, which is probably better anyway since you always *get the wrong end of the stick.*

**B:** That's not true. Anyway, I've tried to warn her about some things, but *it goes in one ear and out of the other*. She doesn't listen.

## DOUBLE CHECK 10: Nerves

I'm completely *tongue-tied* at the moment.
And I don't like *speaking off the cuff* to large groups.
And how do you *break the ice*?

## DOUBLE CHECK 11: Parts of the body

**P:** Jean, *can I have a word in your ear*?
**J:** Sure. You look stressed. Have you got something you *want to get off your chest*?
**J:** Well, that probably explains it. You know he's always *talking about you behind your back.*

## DOUBLE CHECK 12: Silly questions

| | |
|---|---|
| 1. What do too many politicians blow? | *their own horn / trumpet* |
| 2. What should politicians always call a spade? | *a spade* |
| 3. What do most politicians beat about or around when asked any questions? | *the bush* |

## DOUBLE CHECK 13: Scrambled idioms

**A:** Did you hear the *latest gossip*?
**B:** No, but I'm sure you'll *keep me posted.*
**B:** You probably *heard it on the grapevine* somewhere.
**A:** Liz *broke the news to me* yesterday on the phone.

## DOUBLE CHECK 14: Let's go *woggling* again

**O:** That Englishman certainly *took us for a ride.*
**R:** Well, *he fed me a line* about his whole qualifications.
**R:** He *was lying through his teeth* when he accepted the job.

## DOUBLE CHECK 15: Your choice again

**B:** I'm glad Pete has left. He *talked a lot of hot* **(A)** *air* and he got on my nerves.
**R:** You're right. He *was* always **(B)** *rabbiting on* about something or other.
**B:** And what I couldn't stand was the bad language. He *swears like a* **(C)** *trooper.*

## CHAPTER 14

### QUICK CHECK 1: Pitfalls for Germans

1. These shoes pinch. I'm afraid these shoes are too **A.** *small.*
2. Could you **B.** *change* these trousers? I need the next size.
3. Tina's always very elegant. She dresses so **B.** *well.*

### QUICK CHECK 2: What to say in these situations

| The problem | What to say |
|---|---|
| Your raincoat is dirty. | I'd like to *have* my raincoat *cleaned.* |
| The skirt doesn't fit, but you want it after all. | Could you *alter* this skirt? |
| The article is a bit too expensive. | Haven't you *got anything cheape*r? |
| You want to send it as a present. | Can you *gift-wrap it?* |
| It's too heavy and your hotel is far away. | Could I *have* this *sent to* my hotel? |

### QUICK CHECK 3: Beef up your word power

| | |
|---|---|
| 1. Can I help you? | What *can I do for you*? |
| 2. I think I was next. | I think it's *my turn.* |
| 3. We need a deposit of 10%. | We *require* a deposit of 10%. |
| 4. When will it be ready? | How long *will it take*? |

### QUICK CHECK 4: One word for four idioms

1. How long will it *take*?
2. What size do you *take*?
3. I'll *take* this cardigan.
4. Do you *take* German marks?

### QUICK CHECK 5: Remember the idiom?

**J:** My God. I'd never have expected it. Rob seems to be really *down at heel.*
**L:** I think he's wearing *hand-me-downs.*
**J:** Something's happened. He was never short of a bob or two. And all his clothes were *tailor-made.*
**L:** I bet he's gone bankrupt.

## QUICK CHECK 6: Silly questions

| | |
|---|---|
| 1. How should a suit fit you? | *like a glove* |
| 2. What do fine feathers make? | *fine birds* |
| 3. He looks as if he was dragged through what? | *the hedge backwards* |

## QUICK CHECK 7: What's the *woggle*?

**A:** Look at this lovely dress. And *it's going for a song.*

**B:** What do you want to buy clothes for? You won't fit them next week the way you're losing weight. And it's typical of you to *jump at every offer* you see.

**A:** That's not fair! It's a *throwaway price*. And you're only jealous about my weight.

**B:** Okay, okay. I must admit the dress *suits you to a T.*

## QUICK CHECK 8: Animal idioms

1. I'd see the car first. I'm not going to buy a *pig* in a *poke.*
2. I can't afford a Rolls Royce. It's a *white elephant.*
3. Don't look a *gift horse* in the mouth.
4. Fine *feathers* make fine *birds.*

## QUICK CHECK 9: Correct the mistakes

It means our copiers cost *an arm and a leg* in the US. And now our sales department has *jacked / hiked* up the *prices* again. That's the next *smack* in the face.

## QUICK CHECK 10: Take a vowel for an x

**T:** I think you've been *sold a pup.*

**A:** The salesman told me he'd *sold it at a loss.*

**T:** He's *pulled the wool over your eyes!*

## QUICK CHECK 11: Tim, the 'yes-man'

**1.**

**Tom:** Tina wants to buy that pent house from the White Elephant Agency. I'm afraid the prices of property have *risen very rapidly.*

**Tim:** Yes, I know. Property prices have gone *through the roof.*

**2.**

**Tom:** She thinks that penthouse is an *exceptional opportunity.*

**Tim:** Yes, she thinks it's the *chance* of a *lifetime.*

**3.**

**Tom:** She'll pay *far too much money* for a house in that neighbourhood.

**Tim:** She'll pay *through the nose* for a house in that area.

**4.**

**Tom:** And the repairs alone will *cost a large sum of money.*

**Tim:** The repairs will cost an *arm* and a *leg.*

**5.**

**Tom:** I suppose her fiancé *forced her to* buy it.

**Tim:** Sure. Her fiancé must have *railroaded / talked* her into buying it.

**6.**

**Tom:** Poor Tina! The White Elephant Agency will sell her *a house that is worth much less than the price she'll pay for the repairs.*

**Tim:** Yes, they will sell her *a white elephant.*

## CHAPTER 15



### QUICK CHECK 1: Hard times

1. Tom works *full-time.*
2. Tina can work *flexitime.*
3. Anne can work *part-time.*
4. John wanted *to work / do overtime.* He needed the money.

### QUICK CHECK 2: The little difference

1. A bank clerk is a *white collar worker.* He has a desk job.
2. A mechanic is a *blue collar worker.* He works on the shopfloor.
3. A police officer is a *civil servant.* He is employed by the government.

### QUICK CHECK 3: First rungs of the career ladder

1. You *apply* for a scholarship.
2. You *enrol* at a university.
3. You *take* your degree.
4. You *choose* a career.
5. You *send* your application to several companies.

### QUICK CHECK 4: Tim, the 'yes-man'

1. **Tim:** Yes, they have a *vacancy* for a chemist with experience.
2. **Tim:** Yes, I'm sure his friends will help him to *land this job.*
3. **Tim:** Yes, they offer *good prospects.*

### QUICK CHECK 5: Odd man out

1. **Wrong: C.** for a money increase
   **Right:** He went to his boss and asked **A.** for a pay rise **B.** for a wage increase.
2. **Wrong: B.** receive his pension
   **Right:** If the boss said 'no' he would **A.** announce that he is going to leave the firm **C.** give in his notice.
3. **Wrong: A.** tax level
   **Right:** So his boss promoted him to the next higher **B.** wage bracket **C.** income bracket.

15

## QUICK CHECK 6: Find the third man

| pay | |
|---|---|
| wages | salary |

## QUICK CHECK 7: Pitfalls for Germans

1. Tom is *a member* of a Trade Union.
2. Jim is *looking for* a job. He's ready to accept any job.
3. Tom has been out of work *for three months* now.

## QUICK CHECK 8: Beef up your word power

| | |
|---|---|
| be unemployed | be *out of work* |
| be fired | be *dismissed* |
| demand better conditions | *request* better conditions |

## QUICK CHECK 9: What's it in English?

Two apprentices:

**A:** Do you reckon this training is worth anything? As soon as you *get your hand in* they put you on a new job. Then you forget the other skill.

**B:** You're right, of course, but we've all *got to start small*. And then there's the question of the exams.

**A:** Yes, if you don't *pass them with flying colours*, you don't get taken on.

## QUICK CHECK 10: Let's go *woggling* again

**R:** Yes, it was difficult to find anybody. We had to *contact a head-hunter*.

**T:** Well, I wouldn't have employed him. I don't think he's *up to the mark.*

**R:** I know, but good workers are *far and few between*, so I took the risk. Maybe he's *cut out for* this type of work.

## QUICK CHECK 11: What is it?

1. These are typical *perks.*
2. Small number of candidates for a job, etc, selected from a larger number, and from which the successful candidate will be selected: draw up a *short list.*
3. Be of the required standard: *Be up to the mark*

## QUICK CHECK 12: Body idioms

1. Tom's a dab *hand* at trouble-shooting computer problems.
2. He has data processing at his *fingertips.*
3. He's often up to his *eyes / neck* in work.
4. But he's always ready to work his *fingers* to the bone.

## QUICK CHECK 13: What is the second part of the body?

1. Ron is involved heart and *soul* in his work.
2. They're head and *shoulders* above the rest.
3. And they work hand in *hand* with their partners.

## QUICK CHECK 14: Troubleshoot the idioms

**O:** You certainly *know the ropes.*
**A:** I'm *snowed under with work.*
**O:** And in some way you're treated as the *dog's body.*
**A:** I'll just *keep my nose to the grindstone* and it'll be alright.

## QUICK CHECK 15: Animal idioms

1. If you appoint the wrong man for the job you set the *fox* to keep the *geese.*
2. Incompetent workers often put the cart before the *horse.*
3. Lazy bones tend to work at a *snail's* pace.

## QUICK CHECK 16: Let's go *woggling* again

**U:** We're not going to *move a muscle* to finish that job unless you discuss overtime with us again.
**P:** If you don't get on with it, you can all go and *sign on.*
**U:** Are you threatening us? Okay lads, *down tools.* Let's go and *have our elevenses.*
**P:** It'll not be the last you hear of this. Don't *bite the hand that feeds you!*

## QUICK CHECK 17: Remember the idioms?

**M:** You want to *give* Johnson *the push*? Are you sure it's the right decision?
**P:** We have to *axe someone* and he's my first choice. He's a lazy so-and-so.
**M:** He's been here a long time. He'll have to get more than a *leaden handshake.*

| | |
|---|---|
| absent-minded | *zerstreut* |
| accelerator | *Gaspedal* |
| account; take into ~ | *berücksichtigen* |
| ad | *Annonce* |
| adolescent | *Jugendliche / -r Heranwachsende / -r* |
| advertisement | *Werbung* |
| adviser | *Berater* |
| air conditioner | *Klimaanlage* |
| amount to | *sich belaufen auf* |
| announce | *an-, verkünden* |
| apart; fall ~ | *auseinander fallen* |
| apologise | *sich entschuldigen* |
| approach | *sich nähern* |
| argue | *sich streiten* |
| aversion | *Abneigung* |
| avoid | *vermeiden* |
| bachelor | *Junggeselle* |
| bargain | *Geschäft, Handel* |
| be able to afford something | *sich etwas leisten können* |
| be locked in fond embrace | *in zärtlicher Umarmung eng umschlungen* |
| beautician | *Kosmetiker(in)* |
| bother | *belästigen, ärgern* |
| brag about | *prahlen mit* |
| brake pedal | *Bremspedal* |
| brand | *Marke* |
| bribe | *bestechen* |
| bride | *Braut* |
| brothel | *Bordell* |
| buck | *Dollar* |
| cattle | *Vieh* |
| chase | *jagen* |
| cheek | *Backe; Frechheit* |
| cloud-cuckoo land. | *Wolkenkuckucksheim* |
| coalmine | *Kohlebergwerk* |
| coffin | *Sarg* |
| comparison | *Vergleich* |

| | |
|---|---|
| complain | *sich beschweren* |
| complaint | *Beschwerde, Reklamation* |
| contagious | *ansteckend* |
| contest | *Wettbewerb* |
| credit | *gutschreiben* |
| critic | *Kritiker* |
| cuisine; local ~ | *heimische Küche* |
| dashboard | *Armaturenbrett* |
| Dead Sea | *Totes Meer* |
| deadline | *Liefertermin* |
| delicious | *köstlich* |
| delighted | *entzückt* |
| detest | *verabscheuen* |
| diameter | *Durchmesser* |
| digest | *verdauen* |
| dislike | *Abneigung* |
| distribute | *verteilen* |
| do the dishes | *Geschirr spülen* |
| donate | *spenden* |
| drawer | *Schublade* |
| dry-clean | *chemisch reinigen* |
| editor | *Herausgeber* |
| employ | *an- / einstellen* |
| encounter | *treffen, begegnen* |
| estates | *Anwesen* |
| exploit someone | *jemanden ausbeuten* |
| faint | *ohnmächtig werden* |
| favourite | *Lieblings-* |
| fee | *Honorar* |
| figure out | *herausfinden* |
| flu | *Grippe* |
| funeral | *Beerdigung* |
| fuss | *Aufregung* |
| get rid of something | *etwas loswerden* |
| glasses | *hier: Brille* |
| glazier | *Glaser* |

| | |
|---|---|
| grand piano | *Flügel* |
| gratitude | *Dankbarkeit* |
| grave | *Grab* |
| guess | *raten* |
| guilt | *Schuld* |
| handy man | *Handwerker* |
| hanger | *Kleiderbügel* |
| hesitate | *zögern* |
| hiccup | *Schluckauf* |
| hiss | *zischen* |
| host | *Gastgeber* |
| inquire (British E.: enquire) | *sich erkundigen* |
| instead | *anstatt* |
| insulting | *beleidigend* |
| investigation | *Untersuchung* |
| item | *Artikel, Ware* |
| jealous | *eifersüchtig* |
| juror | *Geschworene / -r* |
| label | *Aufschrift* |
| liar | *Lügner(in)* |
| liver | *Leber* |
| lobster | *Hummer* |
| meanwhile | *inzwischen* |
| medical care | *ärztliche Versorgung* |
| mention | *erwähnen* |
| moderate | *gemäßigt* |
| mutter | *murmeln* |
| order | *Bestellung* |
| ordinary people | *Durchschnittsmenschen* |
| overtime | *Überstunden* |
| oxygen | *Sauerstoff* |
| oyster | *Auster* |
| painful | *schmerzlich* |
| pale | *blass* |
| parking tickets | *Strafzettel* |
| pecker | *Nase; Zinken* |

| | |
|---|---|
| pest | *Ekel, Nervensäge* |
| pledge | *Schwur, Gelübde* |
| plumber | *Klempner* |
| postpone | *aufschieben* |
| pregnant | *schwanger* |
| prescription | *Rezept* |
| pretend | *vorgeben; so tun, als ob* |
| printer | *Drucker* |
| prodigal son | *der verlorene Sohn* |
| purchase | *Kauf* |
| quarrel | *Streit* |
| racial discrimination | *Rassendiskriminierung* |
| raise | *erhöhen* |
| reasonable | *vernünftig* |
| rebate | *Rückvergütung; Rabatt* |
| recent | *kürzlich* |
| recognise | *wiedererkennen* |
| recover from | *sich erholen von* |
| refreshments | *Erfrischungen* |
| relieved | *erleichtert* |
| request | *verlangen* |
| revenge | *Rache* |
| Reverend Mother | *Mutter Oberin* |
| review | *Buchkritik* |
| reward | *Belohnung; Entgelt* |
| run out of bread | *kein Brot mehr haben* |
| Salvation Army | *Heilsarmee* |
| share | *Anteil; teilen* |
| smack; get a ~ on the nose | *eins auf die Nase bekommen* |
| solemn | *feierlich* |
| spill | *verschütten* |
| spinach | *Spinat* |
| split up | *sich trennen* |
| spotless | *fleckenlos rein* |
| squirrel | *Eichhörnchen* |
| steep | *überteuert* |

# Word aid

| | |
|---|---|
| Stock Exchange | *Aktienbörse* |
| stomach | *Magen* |
| strand | *Strähne* |
| suggest | *vorschlagen* |
| suspicious | *argwöhnisch, misstrauisch* |
| targeted attacks | *gezielte Angriffe* |
| tombstone | *Grabstein* |
| trust | *Stiftung* |
| unimpressed | *unbeeindruckt* |
| venison | *Rehfleisch* |
| wallet | *Brieftasche* |
| weight | *Gewicht* |
| well-preserved | *gut erhalten* |
| will | *Testament* |
| witness | *Zeuge* |